MW01251259

Visiting Mighty Niagara

**See its Sights, Soils, and Stones
Hear its Stories**

Bill and Gord Jones
Licensed Guides

Visiting Mighty Niagara

Visiting Mighty Niagara

See its Sights, Soils, and Stones
Hear its Stories

Bill and Gord Jones
Licensed Guides

CHI RHO

ChiRho Communications

Visiting Mighty Niagara

See its Sights, Soils, and Stones
Hear its Stories

Bill and Gord Jones
Licensed Guides

CHI RHO

ChiRho Communications

Cover photo: Horseshoe Falls and Table Rock
by **William H. Jones** ©
wmhjones@gmail.com

Table of Contents

The Rainbow Bridge and a Very Wet Canadian Flag

Visiting Mighty Niagara

Introduction

Niagara is a name known throughout the world. The name Niagara stems from the Native name, "Onguiaahra," which is pronounced "on-ge-a-ra." It means "strait," or "throat," and is a symbol of might, power, majesty and beauty. Its origins go to the ice age. Its beautiful awe was respected by aboriginal people long ago. Today, millions of people visit Southern Ontario as tourists, with a priority plan to view and hear Niagara Falls.

Yes, to *hear* the Falls! Some sightless visitors love listening to the roar of the fast flowing rapids leading to the Falls and then onto the Falls itself. The sound of thunder accompanying the mist's water droplets allows blind people to imagine what the Falls really look like. Add to that hearing sense is the mist which, when the wind shifts, can seem like warm summer rain.

If you are sightless, at least you can hear the famous cataract and feel the delightful dampness generated from the cascade. There is a false saying that, "A person who has been to the Falls has seen the mist; a person who has not been to the Falls has missed the scene." You can hear the Falls and feel the Falls even if you cannot visibly see the Falls.

Niagara not only has "mighty large." It also has "mighty small." The 2,000, 175 species emerging butterflies released each morning in the Butterfly Conservatory in their own way are every bit as awesome as the great cascade. We get used to admiring *big*; we need also to acclaim *tiny*.

Moreover, there is much more to Niagara than the Falls, even if the cascade dominates the reasons for visiting the area. The Niagara Parkway is pristine parkland, kept that way by an overseeing body known as the Niagara Parks

Commission (NPC). The NPC maintains the many parks, pays for its own garbage collection and police force. It licenses its guides and requires them to pass an information qualifying test every year.

The NPC receives no government funds; its activities are financed from profits made through tourist outlets at NPC-sponsored shops along the Parkway, i.e., at Table Rock, the Aerocar and several other outlets. Tour busses pay a fee to drive on the Parkway. A portion of a ticket you buy for various highlights, such as the Journey Behind the Falls or the golf courses goes to the NPC. It is a unique way of recompensing the manicured environment of

Niagara on the Lake: Gazebo at Queens Royal Park

the flower gardens, parks and road repairs.

The Niagara Parkway extends along the Niagara River from Fort Erie near Buffalo at the south end, along the River to the Falls, past the Great Niagara Gorge, the Whirlpool, Beck I and II Power Generating Stations, down past the monument to Major General Sir Isaac Brock and north past the escarpment to Niagara-on-the-Lake. The drive along the Parkway is beauteous and restful. It ends at the quaint Niagara-on-the-Lake, decorated with its street lamp poles and their flower pots in its faux old fashioned appearance. Nearby is a newly restored version of Fort George once burned down by American invaders.

If you want to see samples of unique geology, the Niagara area can provide that in spades. Perhaps agriculture intrigues you. Niagara is bountiful in that area too, especially with tender fruits – cherries, peaches, apricots, pears, plums, apples and grapes. A major research station at nearby Vineland provides scientific studies to improve the crops and protect them from infestations. Vineland's research scientists work through the University of Guelph, Ontario.

Niagara history is worth checking out too. You can find out how the Niagara area played a foremost part in unifying Canada during the 1812 – 1814 war that developed with the invasion of Canada by the United States.

The Canadian part of the battles was a sidebar in the main war between Great Britain and France. Yet it cemented the desire of those dwelling in Canada to foster their own national ambitions. Niagara area battlegrounds are celebrated by plaques and in memories of those who gave their lives for king and country, and for unifying a nation.

We must include seeing the Welland Canal. Opened in 1933, it has eight locks, three of which are double flight locks for lifting higher or lower and allowing two-way traffic. The premium views are at Lock Seven and Lock Three. Lock Three also has a good observation area, a video of the canal's history, a mini shop, a museum and brochures of the area's points of interest. A new canal is planned.

This book is about Canada and the spellings are Canadian (somewhere between Webster and the Oxford English Dictionary). You can cope with the spelling.

About the writers . . .

Bill and Gord Jones are brothers and also licensed tour guides in the Niagara Parks area and Toronto. Bill was born in and dwells in Toronto. Bill had the good fortune to marry Glee who was born in Vineland ON, near Niagara Falls. Her father (Dr. W. H. Upshall) directed the horticulture experimental station, now a part of the University of Guelph.

Gord, also born in Toronto ON, specialized as a geography teacher in Niagara Falls. He married Doreen, the daughter of a renowned apiarist (Norm Dyment) in Smithville ON near Niagara Falls. Gord lives in Niagara Falls. He is relatively fluent in Spanish. Both Bill and Gord are graduates of McMaster University in Hamilton, Ontario.

Bill (left) Gord (right)

Chapter One

Where the Niagara Escarpment Stops and Starts

Geological Formations, Glaciers and Erosion

Tourists ask, "How much water flows over the Falls in a minute?" The answer is enough to fill a million bathtubs, or six million cubic feet (168,000 m3). Remember that the Great Lakes (264,000 square miles [684 sq kms] hold 20% of the world's fresh water and the downward flow from five of six Great Lakes is channelled to the Falls from Lake Erie, and the Niagara River. The flow plummets over the brink, then rushes downstream through the class six rapids (highest category) in the world.

Technically, three falls exist. The "tiniest" of them is the Bridal Veil Falls, separated from the American Falls by the 100 ft-wide Luna Island. Its crest line is 50 feet [15 m].

The American Falls, from Prospect Point to Luna Island, is 850 feet wide [260 m]. The drop to the Tallis slope is 70–110 feet [21–34 m] depending on where it is measured.

Present Day Niagara Falls

The Horseshoe Falls, stretches 2,200 feet [670 m] at the brim and descends 177 feet [54 m] to the Niagara River. Below the Falls, the river depth is 185 feet [56.6 m].

During the evenings the water measurements over the Falls drops. It is diverted on both sides of the river through intake towers above the Falls into water channels.

The channels, in turn, refill the Canadian and American reservoirs above the penstocks of the Adam Beck (and Robert Moses) hydro generating stations downstream. The US generation station uses pumps to fill the reservoirs. The pumps reverse to become turbines. Since the land heights viz a viz the descending Niagara River are greater distances apart than upstream, the penstocks offer more power generation to the turbines below.

The rapids generate a whirlpool (see page 19) immediately after the flow opens to a wide bay. Water from the rapids travels counter-clockwise around the bay, descends under the visible water, and rises to enter the continuing northern flow of the Niagara River into Lake Ontario. The eddy is dangerous. A few power boats risk entering the whirlpool without capsizing. Passengers are likely to get wet.

How did Niagara Falls form? What caused the Niagara Escarpment? In a way, the term "escarpment" may be a misnomer. Most escarpments are formed around fault lines where one block has dropped so that the top layer of rock is the same as the section that has "dropped."

A better word for Niagara Escarpment may be the "Niagara Cuesta." It is essentially an erosional feature where first, the softer rock layers erode. Then the cap rock, without much support, falls below. The material is sent by the Niagara River to be deposited elsewhere. It enters downstream into lakes, other rivers, and seas.

The Niagara Escarpment (Cuesta) stretches from New York State to Southern Ontario's Georgian Bay in Lake Huron. It is also in northern parts of Michigan, under Lake Michigan rising at Green Bay, Wisconsin. Its horseshoe-shape faces east in Ontario and faces west in Wisconsin, a distance of over 1,900 kms, [more than 1,060 miles].

The Escarpment is higher in elevation near its edge, in parts over 900 ft [300 m]. It dips to about 550 ft near the Falls. Geologists call the edge, "the scarp face," and the slope, "the dip slope." It comprises layers of compressed materials which come from the Appalachian Mountains to the east of the Allegheny Plateau. They would have been the foothills of the mountains. The rising of the seas and the subsequent run-off provided this material to be compressed into layers of sedimentary rocks.

Fossils, like the sea lily or cup coral (crinoids), indicate that the temperature of the seas 400,000,000 years ago were warm. Limestone, compressed sea shells, would also indicate this.

The "dip slope" of the Escarpment at the Niagara River

The Escarpment (Cuesta) was part of a large dome, most of which has eroded and the present erosion takes place by the rivers and streams flowing over the Escarpment (Hamilton alone has 72 waterfalls). These rivers and streams provide us with manifold waterfalls in the Niagara area.

The Niagara River flows northward from Lake Erie to Lake Ontario, capturing waters from five of the six large lakes in the Great Lakes system (L. Superior, L. Michigan, L. Huron with Georgian Bay, L. St. Clair, and L. Erie. After passing over the Falls, these waters flow northeast through Niagara River into L. Ontario thence to the St. Lawrence River and Atlantic Ocean. Sea level is just past Quebec City.

As with the Niagara River, the Twelve Mile Creek has been used for hydroelectricity (DeCew Falls). In earlier days, these rivers were mainly used for milling grain.

The cap rock of the Escarpment, known as Lockport Dolomite, formed during the Silurian Seas, is made up of calcium magnesium carbonate. Because of its hardness it is

Christ Anglican Church on Niagara Falls' River Road used Dolomite Stone for building

extremely useful for building blocks and stone walls in the area and elsewhere. The protective railing wall along Niagara's River Road is another example of dolomite.

H. A. Tipton's book, *Our Romantic Niagara*, offers examples of many buildings using this quarried stone.
- Locks of the second Welland Canal
- Stone towers of the railway suspension bridge at the foot of Bridge Street in Niagara Falls
- Lewiston (NY) Artpark
- Hamilton Post Office
- Canada House in London, England
- Oak Hall in Niagara Falls
- Court House in Niagara-on-the-Lake
- Parts of locks in the Erie Canal at Lockport NY
- Trinity United Methodist Church, Grand Island NY
- Brock's 1833 and 1859 Monuments at Queenston Heights
- Culverts, tunnels and bridges of the Great Western and Grand Trunk Railways

- Entrance Gate to Rideau Hall, residence of Canada's Governor General in Ottawa
- Ottawa's Parliament Buildings East Block
- Table Rock House in Niagara Parks
- Royal Bank building on Queen St. (NF)
- University buildings at McMaster U in Hamilton ON and Queen's U in Kingston ON
- Christ Church Anglican on River Road, Niagara Falls

Gordon recalls: "In 1968 I went to Queenston Quarries to purchase a stone hearth for my fireplace. The masons quarried it for me and cut the stone into a semicircular form, just as I wanted – a Ukrainian immigrant did the cutting."

Pleistocene (Ice Age) Influences

North America has experience three major "ice sheets." Over time, this action altered the drainage systems. The last glacier was the Wisconsin Ice Sheet, lasting from 100,000 years to about 11,000 years ago.

Not only did the glaciers alter drainage patterns, but they scoured the existing bedrock. They filled in existing gorges as they retreated. They also widened valleys. Their meltwaters formed large lakes.

An ice sheet could be more than a kilometre (almost a mile) high. The damage done by such meltwaters was significant. They acted like a sponge rising as it dries after being compressed. Moreover, the land rose in places after the large ice sheet had melted. The south shore of Lake Ontario rose first to change the flow of water to the St. Lawrence River, so that the previous outlets were through the Finger Lakes (NY) region toward the Hudson and

Mohawk Valleys to the Atlantic Ocean. This flow changed drastically.

Other forms of glacial debris formed into moraines (glacial ridges). Large lakes developed, i.c., Lake Iroquois, Lake Tonawanda and Lake Maumee. The shorelines of these former lakes are still evident. For example, York Road and Queenston Road in Niagara-on-the-Lake, and Davenport Road in Toronto just below the Escarpment are examples of the once-beach of Lake Iroquois. From there to the present Lake Ontario lies the glacial ground overburden for a plain 10 kms (six miles) wide and 45 kms (28 miles) long.

Glaciers also carried large boulders and left them on the land as they retreated. In a house at 4851 River River Rd., NF, builders found an "erratic" (gneiss) and incorporated it into the foundation. Carolyn and

A gneiss (striated) rock–an erratic

Gary Burke cut off some of the rock and moved it to their garden (photo above). A buried erratic was found near Niagara Falls Collegiate on Epworth Circle. Some of these erratics are found in the Niagara Gorge.

Erratics are metamorphic or igneous rocks in make-up, lying on top of the newer sedimentary rocks and glacial overburden. A previous channel of the Niagara Gorge along the glacial face (known as St. David's buried Gorge) has been filled with glacial debris allowing the Niagara River to form a new gorge (or strait). When the Niagara River eroded back to that old gorge, it carried off much of the gravel to expose its presence. It caused the emergence of a whirlpool in the present gorge itself (see page 12) as the river turns right on its onward Lake Ontario journey.

Chapter Two

Aboriginal Dwellers

The Six Nations of the Grand River Territory comprises a league of tribal nations made up of the following: Onondaga, Cayuga, Seneca, Mohawk, Oneida and Tuscarora. The various Nations come under the general group called Iroquois.

The Haldimand Proclamation 25 October 1784 granted them a reserve near Brantford. The negations were conducted by Chief Joseph Brant. A group of Mohawks, led by John Deseronto, wanted the granted land to be near the Bay of Quinte in costal central Ontario. Brant remained adamant that the Grand River area was preferred.

Frederick Haldimand was governor of Lower Canada (Quebec) and has a county named after him in Ontario. He was Commander-in-Chief of The Province of Quebec a few short years after British General Wolf captured the francophone province for Great Britain in 1759.

With the American Revolution of 1776, many US aboriginal tribal areas were lost by native people. Great Britain felt obliged to help them relocate. Therefore, in 1784, eight years after the Revolution, and 29 years after the British victory in Quebec, a large tract of land was ceded to the Six Nation people in the Grand River area of Ontario.

The proclamation read in part: "Whereas His Majesty (George III) having been pleased to direct that in consideration of the early attachment to his cause manifested by the Mohawk Indians, and of their loss of settlement which they thereby sustained – that a convenient tract of land under his protection should be chosen as a safe and comfortable

Her Majesty's Mohawk Chapel, Brantford

retreat for them and others of the Six Nations . . . authorize and permit that the Mohawk Nation and others of the Six Nation Indians as wish to settle . . . I do hereby in His Majesty's name (allot) to them for that purpose six miles deep from each side of the (Grand or Ouse) River beginning at Lake Erie and extending in the proportion to the head of said river, which them and their posterity are to enjoy for ever."

The background to that was that a year before the American Revolution, Joseph Brant visited London, England promising that if the Iroquois people allied with the British, they should receive a freehold land grant in Canada. In the US, American colonists confiscated the land of anyone who was a Loyalist. Great Britain compensated Loyalists with cash, whether Indian or non-aboriginal, for some of the losses they suffered in the 1776 American Revolution. Brant, in 1783, chose the region of the Ouse (Grand) River.

The British purchased this land from the Mississauga tribe and ceded it for Brant's people but did not purchase the land "to the head of the said river." Had the Mississaugas sold all that land, it would have included the present cities of Cambridge, Kitchener and Waterloo. The ceded land for the Six Nations measured 674,910 acres.

Brant argued that his "freehold" land could be sold. He did just that, auctioning off some of the land (381,332 acres) to speculators. In turn, the speculators failed to meet their payments, so Joseph Brant sold more property. Opposing these property transactions was Colonel John Graves Simcoe, lieutenant governor of Upper Canada. That didn't bother Brant.

Governor Haldimand also bought land near the Bay of Quinte and gave it to Mohawks. Some 200 followers of John Deseronto made home there and settled. The town was named after him. The Mohawk name is Tyendinaga.

Meanwhile, Joseph Brant gave away land along the Grand River. Not only did most of the Six Nations settle there, but also 400 native people from other tribes including Cherokee, Tutelo, Delaware and Nanticoke. A 1785 census included: 448 Mohawk, 381 Cayuga, 245 Onondaga, 162 Oneida, 129 Tuscarora, and 78 Seneca.

Additionally, some white families rooted here. They included former members of Brant's Volunteers and Butler's

ST. PAUL'S

HER MAJESTY'S ROYAL CHAPEL OF THE MOHAWKS

Since 1785

On Six Nations of the Grand River Territory

Rangers. (Butlersburg was an early name for Niagara-on-the-Lake). Brant's land largesse created considerable complaint from many aboriginal people who described Chief Brant as an Apple Indian, "Red on the outside, white on the inside." The epithet had some background. He built a sprawling two story European style house, became an Anglican, and served as a "Worshipful Master" in an early Masonic Lodge.

The largest community in the Six Nation's territory was called "Brant's Town," today's Brantford. In 1828, his son John became a chief, serving his people as "an appointed superintendent" for the Six Nations of the Grand River.

However, Six Nations people today are less than satisfied that the terms of the Haldimand Proclamation were fully applied. There remains an ongoing discontented rumble among the aboriginals – a matter yet to be resolved by Canadian politicians and the Six Nations people.

Six Nations Flag   **City of Thorold Flag at Beaver Dams Battleground**

Chapter Three

French and English Occupations

French explorers began to travel west from what Sieur de Champlain called Hochelaga (Montreal) in New France (later, Lower Canada or Quebec). Champlain himself made several forays into what is now Ontario and establish forts for trading purposes. Along side him were the "Charcoals," the Roman Catholic priests who, with a genuine missionary concern, believed that the native people needed a different kind of spirituality.

Champlain didn't need to deal with boundaries, only different tribes or native ethic groups. He soon discovered that the various tribal nations were fearful of each other. Some native people were neutral, wanting to live without war or political connection, simply living off the land. Other natives resented the arrival of the explorers and harassed them.

Étienne Brulé (1592–1633), one of New France's best explorers came from France at age 16. Champlain befriended him, asking him in 1610 to live among the Huron tribe to learn their language and customs. In this way he educated the traders in understanding the Hurons. He also lived among the courrieurs du bois, ("runners of the woods"), living native style off the land. He opened some routes for French fur traders.

His explorations included a route south through what is now the Humber River at Toronto. Among his connections was a Roman Catholic priest, Father Brébeuf (1593–1649), who lived among the Hurons at what is now Midland,

Ontario. Brébeuf attempted to translate "Jesus" into Huron-speak. "God" became "the mighty Gitchi Manitou."

Brulé fell out of favour with Champlain who claimed he assisted the British in developing fur-trading routes. Brulé the explorer return to live among the Huron people who eventually killed him. Sixteen years later, Native people also scalped and executed the Charcoal, Fr. Brébeuf.

French pioneers slowly began to settle in the region of Lake Ontario, although most of them stayed close to New France (Quebec). A few gravitated to the Niagara area. In 1675 a Franciscan priest who had both a missionary and exploration spirit, journeyed to Niagara Falls.

He was the Belgian Father Louis Hennepin. He viewed the Falls and wrote about it in 1678 when some native people brought him to the cataract. He exaggerated what he saw, averred that the Falls was considerably higher than in actuality and claimed that, "The universe does not afford its parallel." Was he the first European to see the Falls? Probably.

The British factor soon became part of New France's interests. The French erected fortifications along Lake Ontario. One of them was Fort Niagara, constructed in 1726 at the northeast side of the Niagara River. It was an impressive structure then and still is, as a tourist museum.

In 1759, Great Britain won a war with France and New France became prize of war. Fort Niagara came under British ownership (by the Treaty of Versailles) until the American revolution. English, not French, became the language of North America except for "Lower Canada" (Quebec) where Great Britain in a generous, conciliatory way, allowed French to be spoken alongside English.

Visiting Mighty Niagara

Fort Niagara NY, formerly French, formerly British, now American

Then came the American Revolution in 1776. Not all Americans having moved to Canada were excited about it. A number of them had migrated north to Canada to live under their preferred British rule.

Some American migrants to Canada were Mennonites who rejected war. A book on their migration is titled, *The Trail of the Black Walnut*. Some stayed in the Niagara area, others journeyed north to what would become Berlin (Kitchener). In Canada the peace-loving Mennonites refused to fight the American invaders. Yet they were stable, fair-minded pioneers who knew how to farm and enrich Canada in so many ways. They too suffered much under the American intrusion of 1812—1814.

Another group of US migrants came to Canada forming a social and political group known as United Empire Loyalists (UEL). When they signed documents, they added UEL after their signatures. They wanted no repeat of an

at Fort George American Revolution. To them, the revolution brought disorder and a reign of irresponsibility. They didn't trust the new American management. Once they arrived and settled in Canada, they helped the British during the War of 1812–1814.

Check the Drummond Hill Cemetery on Lundy's Lane in Niagara Falls, and you will find gravestones marking the UEL settlers. Before the invasion of 1812, American war plotters thought American immigrants to Canada would delight in a US invasion. Some did – but not most immigrants (especially "blacks"). They didn't want what they purposely had left behind.

Fur Traders

Chapter Four

Settlements in and Around Niagara

First the French and then the English settlers moved in among and alongside native peoples who previously had established communities in the Niagara area. From a cave (Cave Springs) along the Niagara Escarpment near Beamsville, some Indian scouts carefully watched Native People of threatening tribes, canoe along the south shore of Lake Ontario.

Soon, the migrating European pioneers moved into the area. They copied many Continental-type communities, setting up their own villages along the southern shore of Lake Ontario and the banks of Niagara River. When the American Revolution began in the mid-1770s, a further English-speaking US migration joined the other immigrants. As noted earlier, these latter migrants were termed United Empire Loyalists (UEL).

Lewiston NY: Monument to escaping slaves about to cross the Niagara River

Loyalists, as the name implies, brought a basic principle with them as they immigrated to Canada. Two centuries earlier, Henry VIII ruled England under the banner know as "the divine right of kings." This was the principle: God permitted the king to rule. God allowed the king to make the rules. By the time of the American Revolution this precept had been watered down, but its last vestiges were firmly set in the minds of some colonialists.

Among the Loyalist immigrants was Colonel John Butler. He was born in New London, Connecticut, and became an Indian agent. He joined the army, rose in rank through lieutenant, then captain. When the 1776 Revolution broke out, he sided with the British and made his way to Quebec. British forces promoted John Butler to major and eventually assigned him to Fort Niagara. American forces wanted to destroy all of the Six Nations working with the British, but Butler opposed this tactic. He had a great affection for native people, knew their languages and their dispositions. He formed the "Butler's Rangers" to protect them and to raid some American bases.

He was assigned eventually to the Canadian side of the Niagara River. He built a barracks for his Rangers (the location may be seen in Niagara-on-the-Lake). From 1781, the community bore his family name, Butlersburg.

Governor Haldimand influenced his promotion to Lieutenant Colonel to a full Colonel. He became a court justice and speculated in Iroquois land. Butler's health failed and he died in 1796, 20 years after migrating to Canada. His best contribution to Canada was not in military prowess, but in his smoothing relations with the Six Nations.

John Graves Simcoe had commanded the Queen's Rangers during the American Revolution and in the years of

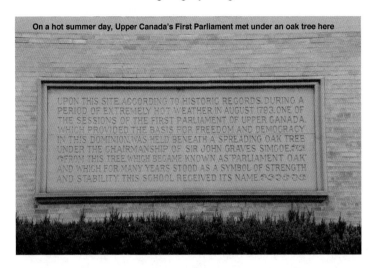

On a hot summer day, Upper Canada's First Parliament met under an oak tree here

UPON THIS SITE ACCORDING TO HISTORIC RECORDS, DURING A PERIOD OF EXTREMELY HOT WEATHER IN AUGUST 1793, ONE OF THE SESSIONS OF THE FIRST PARLIAMENT OF UPPER CANADA WHICH PROVIDED THE BASIS FOR FREEDOM AND DEMOCRACY IN THIS DOMINION, WAS HELD BENEATH A SPREADING OAK TREE UNDER THE CHAIRMANSHIP OF SIR JOHN GRAVES SIMCOE. FROM THIS TREE WHICH BECAME KNOWN AS "PARLIAMENT OAK" AND WHICH FOR MANY YEARS STOOD AS A SYMBOL OF STRENGTH AND STABILITY THIS SCHOOL RECEIVED ITS NAME

British authority, acquitted himself well. When Upper Canada came into existence in 1791–2, Simcoe became Upper Canada's first lieutenant governor and Butlersburg became Newark, a name chosen by the new lieutenant governor, Colonel John Graves Simcoe. Newark was named the capital of the new "province."

Almost his first act as an enlightened governor was to grant land to new American settlers. He believed that in this way they would help develop Upper Canada and would be loyal to British rule. His judgment was correct. When an invasion came, nearly all of the settlers fought against the possibility of American rule – and paid for their loyalty with much suffering from the American invaders.

Lieutenant Governor Simcoe established an Upper Canada parliament in Newark, believing that representation in law-making was "the right thing to do." On a hot summer day, the first parliament met in 1793 in open air, under an oak tree on land now occupied as Parliament Oak School.

The school's exterior wall depicts the first meeting on a frieze facing King Street.

A lake in Ontario is named after his father, and various locations named after Simcoe himself – some streets, a city and a county. There was much reason to honour John Graves Simcoe born in Devon, England. In 1793, he influenced a parliament that made illegal any future slavery. He prevented the New England style of city councils with their excessively rigid covenant-style operations.

He did urge the development of municipal councils, prep schools and universities. Even before Americans threatened to invade Canada, he wisely moved the parliament to York (later called Toronto) as the new capital of Upper Canada (even then Americans burned it). Later, Great Britain appointed Simcoe as Commander-in-Chief for India but he died in 1805 before taking up the post.

Harriet Tubman (formerly Araminta Ross) was a sometime resident of the Niagara region of Canada but she was not a permanent one. Her origins were in Maryland about the time Americans tried to invade Canada at Queenston Heights. Slavery was rampant in Maryland. Harriet's parents were slaves. Her Dad was freed when he was age 45, his freedom bequeathed by his former owner.

Harriet Ross was enslaved when she married a freed black former slave, John Tubman. She used the existing Underground Railroad to reach Pennsylvania, a non-slave state. She commented, "When I had crossed that line, I looked at my hands to see if I was the same person. There was a glory over everything; the sun came out like gold through the trees, and over the fields, and I felt I was in heaven."

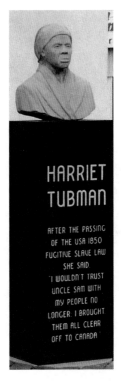

HARRIET
TUBMAN

AFTER THE PASSING
OF THE USA 1850
FUGITIVE SLAVE LAW
SHE SAID
"I WOULDN'T TRUST
UNCLE SAM WITH
MY PEOPLE NO
LONGER. I BROUGHT
THEM ALL CLEAR
OFF TO CANADA

Her longest residency in Canada was about nine months. She helped some of her "passengers" to settle in Canada, mainly in Niagara-on-the-Lake and St. Catharines.

She introduced many other newcomers to Canada's freedom by acting as a determined conductor on the Underground Railroad. Harriet Tubman helped scores of escaping slaves to cross the Niagara River into Canada at both Fort Erie and Queenston. Salem Church in St. Catharines honours her brave, dedicated work with a statue and public display. She claimed to never have run her train off the track nor lost a passenger.

As a result of Tubman's heroic work, many "blacks" found their first freedom in Canada. Decades earlier, some African-Americans had joined the British military, forming the "Coloured Corps," and fought successfully at the Battle of Queenston Heights of 13 October 1812.

Canada's immigration policies left Asians and Jews with little hope of settling in Canada. After WWII, the policies began to change along with more enlightened Canadian attitudes. "DPs" (Displaced Persons) arrived in droves. Knowing what they had gone through, Canadians welcomed them cheerfully often at the docks where they disembarked in Halifax, Quebec City and Montreal. Canadians helped them find jobs and accommodation.

Many Jews who survived the holocaust finally found refugee asylum in Canada. Canada opened its doors to European displaced persons. Asians began to arrive with a warmer welcome offered to them. Nearly all immigrants have made a positive contribution to Canada.

Over the years many Americans migrated to Canada for a variety of reasons. Some came as draft dodgers in the Viet Nam War. Some came to work in the oil industry in Alberta. Some arrived as refugees from Syria. Some came through intermarriage with a Canadian spouse. Some of the draft dodgers later returned to the US and faced their punishment in some cases and amnesty in others. But most remained in Canada and became good citizens.

Canada developed a program of refugee sponsorship. Groups and individuals were able to sponsor those living in refugee camps in parts of Asia and Europe. One example of this is a Toronto Chinese Baptist Church which one year brought 100 "Boat People" from Viet Nam, fed them, housed them, taught them English, shared lives with them and helped them integrate into Canadian Society.

When they arrived on Christmas Day 1979, the church had a feast for them, gifts for them and told them why presents were given at Christmas time. At that gathering one Vietnamese man found that his wife was present. Neither knew whether the other had survived! It was a tearful reunion not just among the newly arriving refugees but also among the Canadian sponsors present. Of that 100, two were Christians, the remainder Bhuddist, showing that there was no bias in the refugee sponsorship.

Chapter Five

Early Tourism and Ice Bridges

Once the French explorers "discovered" Niagara Falls, it took little time for rumours of the great cataract to spread among interested traders. Perhaps Father Hennepin's exaggerated description (see Chapter three) of the cataracts interested tourists in seeing this spectacle.

Europe had nothing like it. The Rhine Falls near Schaffausen may have been the only cataract of any size that Europeans had seen. And the Rhine Falls was no Niagara! It measures 23 m (75 ft) high and 150 m (450 ft) wide.

Where else in the world does such a sight exist or is so accessible to so many people? – so Hennepin thought.

Most people gravitate to the Niagara Region to see the spectacle. Some come for the Clifton Hill neon midway. Stunters, such as Blondin, brought many to watch him risk his life in entertaining them. Others visited the Falls because it is beauteous to behold and the climate is relatively mild.

Before the present Dufferin Islands were created south of the Falls, a vapour sprang from the rocks. Native people were known to strike flints, creating a spark and a fire. It was a vent of methane, rising from the shale below. It received the moniker, "The Burning Spring," in the area of Bridgewater Mills (used for milling wild rice) and was almost as much of a magnetic attraction as the Falls themselves. Well, not quite – but tourists came to see it and paid a token for the privilege.

Two inventive people, Samuel Street and Thomas Clark saw its tourist appeal and advertised the "Burning Spring" in a guide book like this one! They decided to cover the vent with a barrel, by inserting a pipe, then housing it in a building. A manager, M. J. Conklin, collected a minor fee, allowing a visitor into the building. He removed a cork and lit a match, causing a brief flame – thus the "Burning Spring." From June through September, 1884, the manager sold 24,351 tickets of admission. When the area was rearranged into the Dufferin Island Recreation Area, the Burning Spring disappeared or dissipated.

Francis (Fanny) Trollope was one of the early tourists attracted to the Niagara mystique She was a British journalist and writer. She brought her two daughters with her in 1831 and stayed four days. She wrote exuberantly about her visit, concluding, "In short, we strove to fill as many riches of memory with Niagara as possible." Fanny Trollope wrote much more effusively than that but the quote suffices.

She was less effusive about visiting other parts of North America. In her book, *Domestic Manners of the Americas*, published a year after her Niagara visit, she opined on the poor social mannerisms of Americans. She wrote against slavery in, *Jonathan Jefferson Whitlaw*, and greatly influenced the Connecticut writer-abolitionist, Harriet Beecher Stowe. Her children became noted writers.

In 1829, Sam Patch, an entrepreneur from Rhode Island came to Niagara aiming to jump from the Falls for a fee. He chose Goat Island on the US side of the river, near the American Falls. He built a platform 85 feet above the river, jumped and survived.

Not content with his daring Niagara feat, he raised the platform to 125 feet and on 17 October, jumped again – and survived again. Later, he perished in a stunt elsewhere in New York State. Perhaps these exhibitionists led to the early parade of tightrope walkers (see Chapter six, page 41).

Visiting Mighty Niagara

Travelers and tourists translated into the need of overnight accommodation. The war (1812–1814) was not conducive to recreational travel. In 1796, Chippawa had two hotels, Fairbanks House and John Fanning's House. Among the Niagara Falls hotels were Canada House, dubbed "Way Farer's Tavern," and (Charles) Wilson's Tavern. In 1817, William Forsyth bought the hotel from Wilson and renamed it the Prospect Hotel. It changed hands again. He razed Niagara Hotel and replaced with a high ender, three story, Pavilion Hotel with a great overlook of the Falls.

John Brown's stagecoach to (Newark) NOTL and Pavilion Hotel (destroyed by fire 1839) is where he put a chain across the tourist area at Table Rock. Only his patrons had access to the brink. He sent a ship (lake schooner *Michigan* over the Falls as a stunt 1827. The limiting chain was unacceptable to the municipality.

In NY, 1845 General Pankhurst Whitney, proprietor of the Eagle Tavern and subsequently the Cataract Hotel,

A Horseshoe Falls Ice Bridge in the Making

built the Prospect Park Incline Railway, taking tourists from the top of the US side of Niagara Gorge deep down along the Niagara River Gorge. At first, it depended on waterpower to operate but later used electricity. In 1907 a cable snapped, on the railway and sent two railcars to the water's edge.

At the turn of the 20th Century, crowds often descended in winter when the Falls built an ice bridge. Vendors served refreshments on the ice, attracting tourists. The ice cracked, broke up, and three died (Mr. and Mrs. Eldrige Stanton and a would-be rescuer, a youth named Hecock)[1] ending winter excursions on the ice bridge.

One died. Four others were taken on stretchers by the *Maid of the Mist* to the Canadian shore and a Canadian hospital. The Incline Railway operated for 42 years but its run ended with this disaster. Rock slides often stopped the railways from running. During its operation almost a half-million passengers travelled on the Niagara Gorge Railway Company. One severe rock slide destroyed too much track to replace it. Remnants of the track may still be seen at the East (US) side of the Whirlpool (see photo above).

A Canadian railroad competed with its American counterpart because merchants and innkeepers in Canada were losing business to the USA. An electric line was developed to run passengers from Queenston to Niagara Falls ON. Its power was weak, so an auxiliary power plant was built to pull the electric train over the Escarpment hump.

---

[1] Pierre Burton. *Niagara*. Anchor Canada. Toronto. p. 305–6.

Visiting Mighty Niagara

In the summer, the train cars had open sides for travellers to enjoy the sights. They were covered during inclement weather. The trains met the incoming tourist boats from Toronto. In 1932, the Canadian route met the same fate as the American Great Gorge Railway. The Niagara Parkway Commission refused to renew its licence.

In the 1860s a "Shadow of the Rock" attraction was built to allow tourists to reach a platform to experience the mist and thunder of the American Falls.

In due time the *Cave of the Winds* on the American side allowed tourists to scramble down a walkway between the American Falls and the Bridal Veil Falls. In 1910, Americans built an elevator for tourists to reach the base of the American Falls. It closed in 1954.

A new elevator, sponsored by the Niagara Preservation State Park was constructed in 1961 allowing visitors to reach the base of the Falls. Later, officials constructed a Scenic Lookout for visitors to walk "over the edge" and overlook the Niagara River, gaining a better view of American, Bridal Veil and Horseshoe Falls.

At first, stagecoach and train were used to move tourists from Toronto to Niagara Falls and return. But quickly, the most popular way to travel was by lake boat.

In 1827 British steam boats began ferrying tourists and other passengers from York to Niagara Town. The ships were named *City of Toronto* and the *New City of Toronto*. The voyage took 4.5 hours. By 1839 ferry boat service was going "great guns" between Queenston and Toronto. Of course it had no guns (just an expression!). It carried freight and passengers.

By 1878 a group of Toronto entrepreneurs established the Niagara Navigation Company. It operated a fleet of steamships between Toronto, Niagara-on-the-Lake and Lewiston. The initial ship, launched in 1880, a side paddle wheeler, was named *SS Chicora*, built in Liverpool.

In 1878 the Niagara Navigation Company put it into profitable daily service on Lake Ontario between the ports of Toronto and Queenston. A sister ship *SS Cibola* join her in 1888 but burned in Lewiston port. The *Cibola* was replaced by the *Carona*. Another ship, the paddle wheeler *SS Chippewa* (sic) joined the fleet shortly after, in 1894.

Canada Steamships Lines (CSL) took ownership of the ferry service between Toronto, Queenston and Niagara-on-the-Lake. From Toronto through the Eastern Gap past Ward's Island the voyage took about two hours. Morning departure was at 9:15. Picnic hampers packed with lunch goodies to be eaten in the Queenston Heights Park.

A new ship, the *SS Cayuga*, made this run from 1907 to 1959. *Cayuga* was launched in March 1903, capable of ferrying 1,900 passengers across Lake Ontario in style. She became the flagship of the Toronto–Queenston route. It was a two-funnel ship, propelled by two screws (not paddle wheels) and was regarded as a naval architectural treasure.

During WWII, the fare was $1.00 for adults, 50¢ for children (plus a war tax) had dance nights, moonlight cruises and a dance band. In the years from 1907 to 1959, Cayuga carried 15,000,000 passengers. It carried passengers, freight and automobiles to Queen's Royal Park in Niagara-on-the-Lake, Queenston and Lewiston. An electric train met the ship at Queenston and transported passengers south to the Falls.

Both authors of this book will testify that plying Lake Ontario on either the *Cayuga* or the *Chippewa* to the Niagara area was a summer highlight.

Visiting Mighty Niagara

At the height of the boat traffic across the lake, another set of ships toted people from Toronto to Port Dalhousie near St. Catharines. These were the *Dalhousie City* and the *Northumberland*, crossing daily from Toronto to Port Dalhousie twice a day. Port Dalhousie had a park with rides and carousel, so it was a great place to picnic with children. The *Northumberland* was purchased from a company using it in the travelling area of Prince Edward Island, New Brunswick and Nova Scotia. It was the better and faster of the two ships. It later burned.

By 1950, the fate of the lake boats was sealed. During the WWII, Canadians could not buy automobiles as the war effort occupied car factories. With the war over, the pent-up desire for automobiles, together with the (then) "super highway" Queen Elizabeth Way (QEW), allowed cars to reach Niagara Falls in less time than the lake boats. Within 15 years from war-end, the lake boats could no longer compete. Motor cars displaced the ships.

But Niagara Falls did not lose out. In Canada even more attention was paid to the thriving tourist industry. Canada always had the best view of the Falls and everyone knew it. Canada had a full frontal view of the three cataracts. The view from the US side is also mighty impressive. Today, 7,000,000 visitors a year travel to Niagara Falls from every part of the world. You don't believe it? Listen to the languages spoken on your *Hornblower* Cruise or in the hotels and restaurants.

Chapter Six

Daredevils: Barrels and Tightropes

Some people like to tempt fate. In 2013, a young woman taking photos near Table Rock, decided she could get a better "shot" by stepping over the guard rail. We'll never know how the photo turned out. But she had the ride of her life – the last ride of her life.

Some people give no heed to warning or danger signs and they pay for it dearly. Back in 1912, visitors and residents alike flocked to the frozen Niagara River below the Falls. It was done every year since 1900, wasn't it? In 1912, the Falls was embellished by huge mounds of ice, as high as 10 stories, and money was to be made by selling refreshments and entertainment.

The ice bridge suddenly broke that year, and three of the people trapped on the ice bridge were carried to their deaths. No access to the ice bridge has been permitted since then. The ice bridge is now somewhat lessened by barriers upstream to prevent most ice from going through the power intake tower systems.

In the previous century, during the summer of 1859, a famous French tightrope artist, Charles (Jean-François) Blondin, set up his tour de force 160 feet high above the Niagara Gorge, approximately across from where the White Water Walk is located today. Blondin drew large crowds, including The Prince of Wales, the future King Edward VII.

His shtick had many variations. He crossed on stilts, crossed while blindfolded, was in a sack, and sat down partway across to cook and eat an omelet, while standing on a chair and only one leg of the chair on the tightrope. He offered to take someone in a wheelbarrow but had no takers.

He invited the Prince of Wales to join him, but the future king declined, instead giving the acrobat 50 guineas. Once, at least, Blondin carried his manager quaking Harry Colcord on his back across the Gorge on the tightrope. His tightrope was 1,100 feet (340 m) long and 3.25 inches (8.3 cm) in diameter. At age 72 Blondin died of diabetes at his London home he dubbed "Niagara House."

With the Civil War beginning in 1861, the stunting stopped for a long while. In Blondin's story, his stunting in Niagara ended when the Civil War began. Americans became less interested in amusement than in war casualties.

The Niagara Parks Commission has clamped down on what it calls "stunting." The NPC will punish anyone attempting a stunt with a $10,000 fine. However, in 2013, Nik Wallenda, of the famous acrobatic Wallenda family, persuaded the NPC to allow him a televised performance crossing by tightrope from Goat Island in New York, USA to Niagara's Table Rock in Ontario, Canada. The NPC grudgingly acceded to his request, saying it might consider a "stunt" every 20 years.

Niagara Parks Commission's reluctance to allow stunting follows several failures in going over the Falls. The list of successes and flops is as follows:

1. Annie Edson Taylor	24 Oct. 1901	survived
2. Bobby Leach	25 July 1911	survived
3. Charles Stephens	11 July 1920	died
4. Jean Lussier	04 July 1928	survived
5. George Stathakis	04 July 1930	died
6. William "Red" Hill Jr.	05 Aug 1951	died
7. William Fitzgerald PhD	15 July 1961	survived
8. Karel Soucek	03 July 1984	survived
9. Steven Trotter	18 Aug 1985	survived

10. David Munday	05 Oct	1985	survived
11. Peter DeBernardi with Jeffrey Petkovich	27 Sep	1989	survived
12. Jessie Sharp	05 June	1990	died
13. David Munday (2nd time)	26 Sep	1993	survived
14. Steven Trotter (2nd time) with Lori Martin	18 June	1995	survived
15. Robert Overacker	01 Oct	1995	died
16. Kirk Jones	20 Oct	2003	survived

The above stunters used a variety of contraptions to attempt their "going over" the Falls – barrels, inner tubes, kayaks and jet–skis. Whatever works!

One unintended person going over the Falls was Roger Woodward. On 09 July 1960, seven-year old Roger was boating with his sister Deanne in the upper rapids. They were guests of Jim Honeycutt, who worked with their father. Jim's motor sheared a pin.

Deanne scrambled over rocks to reach the riverbank. Roger, wearing a life jacket, went over with the boat and Jim. Roger bobbed in the water below the Horseshoe Falls and was picked up by the unbelieving captain of the Maid of the Mist. Honeycutt did not survive. Woodward later became an industrialist. Both authors have met him.

THE HIGH

HILL'S BARREL
JULY 1949
Used by Major Hill at the Gorge

Chapter Seven

War and Its Participants

The expansionist mood in United States of America was growing in 1812. Not long before, the US had acquired the Louisiana Purchase.

History is complicated but the story is that France, already having lost Canada in 1759, claimed this southern territory (1669–1762), but ceded it to Spain, which ceded it back again to France under Napoleon Bonaparte's conquests.

That was 1800. France wanted to build an empire in North America but could not afford to keep up the costs of running such a large territory.

The Louisiana Purchase incorporated all of Arkansas, Missouri, Iowa, Oklahoma, Kansas, and Nebraska. It also enveloped parts of Minnesota, North Dakota, South Dakota, New Mexico, Texas, Montana, Wyoming, Colorado, and Louisiana. Parts of Alberta and Saskatchewan were a parcel of the purchase but eventually were given to Canada.

Thomas Jefferson, US president, bought the territory from France in 1803 mainly to get French influence out of the USA. He paid $15,000,000 for the land, including debts incurred by France.

Some in the US Congress objected on a matter of constitutional law. Jefferson did not comprehend the size of the territory he acquired, so with funding from Congress, he employed explorers

Lewis and Clark to map out the area.

Jefferson set out his goal for these explorers. It was to find "the most direct and practicable water communication across this continent for the purposes of commerce." Jefferson dictated that the US had sovereign rights over native people along the Missouri River.

Thirteen years after Jefferson's purchase, James Madison was president of the USA. He had served Jefferson as Secretary of State, supervising the Louisiana Purchase, and followed him in the presidency.

During those early presidential years he dealt unsuccessfully to dismiss a British embargo on American ships trading with Britain's enemy, France. Undoubtedly, in dealing with the embargo, he must have mused that Canada was relatively unguarded while British troops were engaged with France. From a Canadian perspective this provided him with an opportunity to add to the Louisiana Purchase by annexing Canada.

So the US invaded Canada, first in southeastern Upper Canada (Ontario). US General Hull was up against a brilliant British general (Brock) who bloodlessly took over Fort Michilimackinac and subsequently tricked US General Hull into surrendering Fort Detroit. Madison court-martialled General Hull (later reinstating him).

But the conflict continued. On 13 October

On the slope where Isaac Brock Died

1812, an American force on several bateau crossed the swift-flowing Niagara River near Queenston, took the Queenston Heights, and fought valiantly, killing Major General Sir Isaac Brock by a sniper's bullet and almost winning the day.

The US invaders didn't count on two realities. One was that the invaders had too few boats to ferry reservist US forces stranded in Lewiston NY and insufficient ammo to continue fighting. The other fact was that they couldn't handle the strategies of the native warriors who courageously pinned down the Americans and forced them to surrender.

American forces continued to fight the British forces, Canadian Militia, and Native Warriors guarding Canada. The two sides fought some battles on water in the Great Lakes and in Quebec. Some other fighting was on land near Detroit and around

London ON.

For purposes of this book, we relate only some of the battles, those where the conflicts found their way into what is now called The Golden Horseshoe, that is, Fort Erie, Niagara, Niagara-on-the-Lake, Beaverdams, Stoney Creek/Hamilton/Burlington, and York (Toronto).

Queenston Heights

The Niagara Region suffered through five serious battles, the first of which was at Queenston Heights. It marked the beginning of two years' conflict with the United States in something of a sidebar to the quarrel the US had with Britain. Britain was annoyed at the US for supplying the French while Britain was at war with Napoleon.

Monument to Alfred, Sir Isaac Brock's Horse

Great Britain embargoed US ships, often press-ganging the crews to serve the British Navy. The US response was to invade Canada and its first objective was to capture the British defensive canon battery on Queenston Heights – the Redan Battery.

The "somewhat" surprise attack came on 13 October 1812. A contingent of American troops, various sources say 6,000, maybe 3,000, assembled at Lewiston NY. The first wave involved 13 bateau, ferrying the first wave of American invaders across the swift-flowing Niagara River. A couple of soldiers could not handle their craft and they went down river. The other troops quickly scaled the hill at Queenston Heights and attacked the British garrison, but not before the defenders spiked the Redan canons so that American soldiers could not use them.

The sound of canon alerted British soldiers upstream and downstream. Led by Major General Sir Isaac Brock they attempted to scale the trail leading uphill to the battle. Brock was killed and so was his Aide-de-Camp, Colonel Macdonell.

Sir Roger Hale Sheaffe took command, and routed his troops to the back of the American positions, successfully advancing on the American fighters. Americans were badly led, ran out of ammunition, and fled from British bayonets and Native scalpers. The timid US reinforcements failed to arrive. They were petrified by the Six Nation natives' war cries. Many Americans died scrambling down the cliff they had ascended so easily the same morning. The 900 surviving American invaders surrendered.

Fort York. Upper Canada Lieutenant Governor John Graves Simcoe had wisely moved his capital from Newark (now Niagara-on-the-Lake) to York (now Toronto). Simcoe had anticipated the signs of war before it started.

On 27 April 1813, the guards at Fort York spotted a flotilla of 16 American warships heading toward them. They were led by Commodore Isaac Chauncey. For two days, the fleet bombarded Fort York and reduced it mostly to rubble. The 1,700 invaders landed west of the Fort and marched toward it. But York had only 700 defenders. General Sir Roger Hale Sheaffe moved his British soldiers in the direction of Kingston and left two militia officers to negotiate a surrender.

The Stolen Mace

What followed was a disaster for the Americans. A fire started or was started in the Fort's magazine. It exploded, hurling stones at the Americans. Between the rocks and the shock waves, 40 men died outright, and another 200 severely wounded men died later.

One US casualty among the many was Brigadier General Zebulon Pike (who gave his name to Colorado's Pike's Peak). He was carried to an American warship, died of wounds, and was buried in a military cemetery at Sacketts Harbor NY. The US forces had thought they would receive a warm welcome from York's inhabitants but their looting in the town discounted any consideration of that.

Before the Americans left, they burned Upper Canada's new Parliament Buildings and stole the Fort's flag and Parliament's mace, the authority which allowed representative members of the Upper Canada to meet and do their parliamentary business.

Battle of Beaver Dams Memorials

Battle of Beaver Dams. The British Lieutenant James FitzGibbon was in charge of British forces stationed at DeCew House near Beaver Dams (close to the present Lock Seven on the Welland Canal).

One wonders if he was more surprised by Laura Secord's appearance in a long dress torn from rushing through underbrush to warn him of an impending battle, or of the audacity of American troops in trying to take the ground he guarded. No matter, he was prepared when the American forces

51

Re-enactment of British/Native People Victory at Stoney Creek 05 June 1813

arrived. That was 12–13 June 1813.

Iroquois warriors friendly to the British had already harassed the Americans as they arrived near Beaver Dams. FitzGibbon rode to meet them with a white flag, warning the Americans that they must surrender or face the Iroquois and a superior British force. The American Colonel Boerstler conceded that surrender was appropriate. Thus the Battle of Beaver Dams resulted in fewer casualties.

Stoney Creek. The Americans gradually changed tactics. They began a burn-and-loot campaign and attempted to increase strength along Lake Ontario's south shore. This battle preceded Beaver Dams.

British forces had retreated to Burlington Heights when American General Dearborn sent

3,700 troops from his now-occupied Fort George to attack the British at Stoney Creek. First, the undisciplined invaders hassled private citizens and looted their homes.

Americans intended to capture Stoney Creek, Burlington, York and eventually Kingston where British forces were more deeply entrenched.

On 06 June 1813, the Americans camped at Stoney Creek when 700 British soldiers and a few Native warriors mounted a 2:00 am surprise attack although the enemy outnumbered them five to one.

The night attack worked. Many US soldiers were asleep when roused by intimidating war hoops made mostly by the British soldiers. The Americans were disoriented, confused and frightened by the war cries. Many were bayoneted. The fight was at close quarters. The invaders fled in disarray.

British troops returned to Burlington Heights lest the Americans figured out how few they were. The battle had lasted most of two days when American troops retreated to "safer" ground.

Soon to follow was an American torching of homes and farms along the south shore of Lake Ontario. By burning houses and crops, the US armies left the Canadian civilian settlers desolate, women and children as well as farmers and merchants, without shelter and with burned crops. They had no way of dealing with the harsh Canadian winter in December 1813 and faced starvation.

The British forces responded by burning everything along the American side of the Niagara River from Fort Niagara to Buffalo.

Later, the British army torched Washington's White House but President Madison had vacated it much earlier. Dolly Madison stayed at the White House until 20 minutes before the British attack.

Chippawa. Americans had imbedded themselves at various points along the Niagara Frontier. On 03 July 1814, they launched a strong attack near Chippawa. This time, a very disciplined US force was more than a match for the well-trained British.

Leading the US attackers was Brigadier General Winfield Scott. He understood the need for good training, good tactics and discipline. In other words, he was a military professional, unlike previous generals in the US invasion forces. Consequently, the superior US force outdid the combined defenders by a wide margin.

Two thousand, one hundred Canadian, Six Nation allies and British regulars faced a superior force of well-trained 3,500 American regulars and their disciplined Native allies.

Over 800 defenders died or were wounded. The defenders retreated to Fort Chippawa located where the Welland and Niagara Rivers meet. The survivors were needed for the next battle at Lundy's Lane three weeks later.

Lundy's Lane. Americans pursued the British, Native and Canadian forces, surrounding the other forts of George and Mississauga. The American fleet failed to arrive with American reinforcements. So on 25 July, the two armies clashed at Lundy's Lane (at present-day Drummond St). About 1,700 fighters on

Drummond Battlefield / Lundy's Lane Cemetery

each side engaged in battle, producing 1,900 men dead and wounded in the six hours of fighting on the one day. The Americans claimed victory but it was the British who remained standing!

Lundy's Lane was not the last battle of the war but it ended the American advance into Canada. A cemetery now at the battle site has graves of many United Empire Loyalists.

Fort Erie. The Americans had captured Fort Erie sometime earlier in 1913, lost it, and recaptured it

03 July 1914. American survivors of the Chippawa and Lundy's Lane battles found refuge in Fort Erie.

The British forces determined to recapture the Fort and began a siege in August 1814. For the British, it was a disaster – 3,000 dead.

But on 12 August the British did capture two US vessels near the Fort on Lake Erie. The attack on the Fort began 13 August with a two day bombardment, and an attack on 15 August.

Attacks were repeated on 17 September. Americans had "fortified" the Fort and experienced less damage than the British expected.

Moreover, British military leaders made some drastic mistakes. Lieutenant Colonel Victor Fischer told his troops to remove their flints lest their guns accidentally discharge. He told them it would be a bayonet attack.

Two other British positions were detected by the Americans. The British were trapped and decimated. A British commander, Colonel William Drummond, was killed.

The net result was that the British lifted the siege. In November, the Americans went back across the river and all fighting in Canada stopped.

The main war participants brokered a peace in Belgium (The Treaty of Ghent) was signed between France and Britain on Christmas Eve, ending and the War of 1812–1814 in Europe and in North America. (The exception was in Louisiana three weeks after peace was signed when the British

forces lost a post-war disastrous battle to Andrew
Jackson). But Canada remained Canada.

Guards prepare their weapons for firing at Old Fort Erie

Chapter Eight

Lasting Peace and Prosperity

Civil War General William Tecumseh Sherman is credited with coining the phrase, "War is hell." That was accurate in the War of 1912–14 also.

War is a thief. It steals your wealth, your children, your plans, your morality and your security. War is a liar; it cannot tell the truth. Stating that war is destructive is a terrible understatement.

Canadians and Americans alike were weary of war. America was just short of bankruptcy and Britain was in financial straits. The imposed peace stemming from the Christmas Eve 1814 Treaty of Ghent was a welcome pact. It was time again for "peace on earth, goodwill to men."

The Western (Ontario) settlements, also the sparsest in population, suffered the most economical damage and took the longest to recover.

Along the Thames River where Americans burned villages and crops, the battered population tentatively began to restore law and order.

Moravian Delawares rebuilt their village but on the opposite side of the river. American thieves returned property they had appropriated, with two exceptions,– the flag and mace that General Zebulun Pike's invaders filched from the new Upper Canada parliament buildings during their 1813 attack at York.

In late 1814 US General Duncan McArthur had advanced to the western edge of the Grand River, today's Brantford but defenders denied him reaching the east side – he couldn't cross it. In the autumn of 1814, with some support from American sympathizers living in Canada, he burned buildings and crops in the First Nations' lands at the west side of the Grand River. He and his troops could not transverse the Grand. This was a revengeful and spiteful act for Duncan McArthur's having surrendered Fort Detroit to General Brock in 1812. With the war over, survivors in the Six Nations territory acted neighbourly and helped each other to recover and rebuild.

Resentment and revenge afflicted traitors. Britain promised reparations for buildings burned, assets seized and crops destroyed. But with its financial position in tatters, British payouts were slow in coming.

Britain did not begin to pay reparations until 1837 – 23 years after the war's conclusion; many claiming war losses had long passed away by then. Niagara area residents claimed the most war reparations.

Burned and pillaged York came off the lightest damaged. The Parliament Buildings were rebuilt. US President Franklin Delano Roosevelt returned the mace in 1937 as "an act of friendship."

He did not return the flag. When British troops captured Fort Niagara in 1814, they took the American flag. Britain returned the flag in 2006 "as an act of friendship."

However, Lady Drummond, a descendent of the General, and possessor of that trophy, tried to clean it before Britain returned the flag. It caught fire. She doused it and put the singed flag in a washing machine. It came out tattered. The well-travelled, charred, threadbare and frayed flag was returned to Fort Niagara in 2006 and now rests in a deserved retirement at a Niagara museum.

Six Nations United

Native peoples made peace with each other, gathering at Burlington for a reconciliation powwow. Not all the native people had sided with the British.

Two of the six aboriginal nations were more empathetic to the United States. But with the peace, British plans for a large Indian territory were scuttled by the peace treaty. The biggest losers in the war were native people.

Brant: Freemason; Warrior; Diplomat; Anglican

The Grand River Indian lands shrunk. The British had granted Joseph Brant and the Mohawk people tracts of land, six miles on each side of the Grand River in Ontario. Chief Joseph Brant learned from the British to drink tea, a habit which many of his tribe detested.

He assisted the British and Foreign Bible Society in translating the first ever translation of Mark's Gospel (into Mohawk) to any language other than English.

What may be an unconfirmed malicious rumour is that Chief Brant drank his way to death and sold much British-granted land to fuel his drinking habit. It is better to think that the rumour is completely untrue, just a "stab in the back" by his numerous critics.

He died before the 1812 War but from his grave he commanded the participation of four of the six nations near Brantford ON. Brantford (Brant's Ford) is named after him (See Chapter two, pages 22, 23).

What About a Canal to Circumnavigate the Falls?

Canada was wary of any future connections with the United States – would the US invade again?

Consequently, and with commercial trade in mind, some entrepreneurs in Canada began to consider building a canal connecting Lake Erie and Lake Ontario. The drop is 326 feet! See the next chapter discussing the Welland Canal).

Bad Blood

An American dissident chose a holy day to disturb Sir Isaac Brock's rest. The first memorial to Sir Isaac Brock was blown up on Good Friday, 1840 by a bitter, malevolent Irish-American, anti-British, Benjamin Lett.

Lett crossed the border and with a keg of black powder and dynamited the imposing monument. This so enraged Canadians that a bounty of £1,000 was placed on his head but never paid because he could not be cornered. Americans somewhat protected him. Even when Lett was arrested, the US did not extradite him.

A year previous, Lett had tried to burn British ships moored in Kingston ON, and even a British ship docked near Oswego NY. He was wanted also in the USA for various felonies including murder, was arrested but escaped.

He died five years later of strychnine poisoning in the midwest USA. Influential Canadians met at Queenston Heights to decide what to do about the desecration of Brock's burial place and the destroyed memorial. They agreed to build a better, bigger "Brock's" monument.

The money was quickly raised, so thoughtful were the donors of a Canadian hero. The new Brock's Monument opened in 1856 with a height of 56 metres (184 feet).

A Need for Alternate Canals

The War of 1812–1814 impacted many events in Canada. One was the need of secure waterways to ensure secure and battle-free trade. In 1832–3 two canals opened to offer safe and non-interrupted passage for goods and personnel in Southern Ontario.

The least urgent of these was the Trent-Severn waterway which began as a canal in the Kawartha Lakes region partly for shipping lumber from sawmills and only partly as a defensive manoeuvre in case the Americans invaded again. In time, the system connected Georgian Bay on Lake Huron to Trenton on Lake Ontario.

The more urgent waterway was a canal for shipping goods and materiel from Lake Ontario (and vice-versa) to what would become the new capital of Canada. Queen Victoria later named Bytown as Ottawa. This canal also served for security and protection from Americans.

The Rideau (named in 1613 by Sieur de Champlain, French for "curtain," or falls) saw construction beginning in 1826. Lieutenant Colonel John By, a British army engineer, supervised the plan and construction.

It became a 125 mile (202 km) river system with 47 masonry locks and 52 dams. The series of canals created a navigable waterway between Kingston and Bytown that offered security and better trade opportunities. Today, the canal is mostly a recreational waterway.

Rebellion

Rebellions sometimes work. Often, the results differ from the objectives of the rebels. Issues relating to governance nagged some citizens following the British victories of the War of 1812–1814. One such rebellion surfaced in Lower Canada (what later was called Quebec) and a twin rebellion arose in Upper Canada (the future

Ontario). Both rebel groups wanted a change from British colonial rule.

The rebellion in Lower Canada, led by Louis Joseph Papineau was less damaging because members of the legislature were sympathetic to his concerns. They opposed the domination of the Roman Catholic Church. They were rebuffed by British leadership when Papineau and his many friends asked the crown to grant more responsible government – true democracy. It didn't help that in the mid 1830s, French Canadian farmers underwent an economic recession.

A mini rebellion created a British and Anglophone backlash, causing the Papineau group to flee for refuge in the USA. They organized a "disorganized" second rebellion (1838) but it too failed.

At the same time, William Lyon Mackenzie fomented a rebellion in Upper Canada, again protesting the lack of democracy, or the dominant preservation of the Family Compact (Anglican privileged domination) under British rule. The Compact was an "old boys" religious network specializing in patronage.

Mackenzie grew tired of asking for change. He gathered about 1,000 "rebels" intent on overthrowing the Upper Canada Parliament and forming a republic. Many of the rebels were rooted in the US and sympathetic to republicanism.

In November 1837, the motley mutineer menagerie met for a half-week in what is now Thornhill ON at Montgomery's Tavern. They marched south on Yonge Street to face an orderly militia. Almost 300 rebels died, along with more than a score of the militia. Another 100 rebels were captured. The surviving insurgents fled to the USA and hid out with like-minded American friends. Later, when the smoke cleared, Mackenzie returned to Canada and eventually was elected as the first mayor of Toronto.

The mini-rebellions fomented some positive consequences. The British Government listened. It appointed Lord Durham to write a report. The ensuing Durham Report recommended uniting the two areas, Upper and Lower Canada, forming The Province of Canada in 1841. This led to truly responsible, representative government.

Thus Canada successfully organized a united two "province" political reality with Louis Hypolite LaFontaine who worked with Robert Baldwin and Francis Hincks to form their united party. Hinks eventually became Minister of Finance in the first John A. Macdonald confederated government of 1867. LaFontaine was in effect, the first prime minister of Canada (the two Canadas). He later became Chief Justice of Canada's Supreme Court.

The Path to Canadian Confederation

Lord Durham's incisive report set the stage for the 1867 confederation of five provinces [Ontario, Quebec, Prince Edward Island (1873), New Brunswick, Nova Scotia] with delegates meeting for three years in Charlottetown PEI.

This culminated in a confederated Canada, 01 July 1867 (PEI excepted until 1873). Other provinces gradually joined: British Columbia, Manitoba, Saskatchewan, Alberta and finally in 1949, Newfoundland/Labrador. Canada also governed three territories, Yukon, Northwest, and Nunuvit.

An early threat to Canadian confederation came from the Fenians, a grumbling group of Irish-Americans and their companion crowd in Canada, the Irish-Canadians. The real issue was the Irish homeland, governed by Great Britain.

Their aim was to liberate Ireland from the British. As in many instances, such as President James Madison's decision to invade Canada in 1812, the Fenians thought they could strike Britain through its British connections rather than by direct confrontation.

One of their leaders in the USA, John O'Mahony, determined to invade Canada. He found sympathy among some Canadians of Irish descent who tried to initiate raids in New Brunswick (April, 1866) and Ontario (01 June 1866).

The group fragmented but not before murdering a newly elected Canadian member of Parliament. Fenians briefly hassled many areas during 1866–8, including Ridgeway Ontario and Missisquoi, Quebec.

A Fenian assassinated D'Arcy McGee MP, the only federal political assassination to date in Canada's history. They attempted a similar coup in Manitoba in 1871 but failed. Their raids did more to cement Canada than to fracture the nation. Eventually, the Fenian discontent gave rise to the IRA in Ireland.

The IT Generation Begins in Brantford

As militant objections to Canada's future began to diminish, business and invention developed. Alexander Graham Bell spent time between Massachusetts, Nova Scotia and Ontario. His research progressed. He believed that the telegraph's advantages could be harnessed to the human voice. Bell had worked on helping deaf people. Bell's research led to the telephone's invention in Brantford.

Bell set up his lab (now a museum) in Brantford, Ontario. First, he sought to improve the telegraph. This developed, with assistance from a young electrician Thomas

Alexander Graham Bell Homestead, Brantford

Watson, into a surprising result. An accident of a reed stuck to an electromagnet, led to a sound and tones.

This surprise led to further experiments. Finally, on 10 March 1876, Bell made the first telephone call to his assistant: "Mr. Watson – come here – I want to see you." The inventor created not only a phone but a company – Bell Telephone. The first telephone office is next to Bell's Homestead. He created much more.

Canada Builds A Railway

The formation of a confederated Canada was dependent on a connecting railroad. The Canadian Pacific Railway (CPR) began in 1881 in Eastern Ontario near Pembroke and was completed on 07 November 1885 when the last spike was driven into the rail at Craigellachie in British Columbia.

British Columbia only agreed to join a confederated Canada if a railway was guaranteed to the west. Later the Canadian Pacific Railway extended east to the Atlantic provinces by 1889. Still later, several other struggling, fledgling railroads amalgamated to form a competitor to the CPR, Canadian National Railways (CNR).

The railway progressed through several iterations, acquiring land and ships in the process. Through its agencies, it sold much land to settlers and homesteaders. The CPR held the fragile nation together, cementing it with excellent, necessary and reliable transportation.

Before long the CPR also founded premiere tourist hotels with cachet in Banff, Winnipeg, Vancouver, Toronto, Ottawa and Quebec City so that patrons of the CPR could have places to stay upon reaching their destinations.

Canada Needs Power

Power creates progress and progress creates power. In post-1812–14 war, Upper Canada/Ontario needed electric power for the new manufacturing generation. Thomas Edison in Menlo Park NJ, showed the world that electrical power was not an option but a necessity. Alexander Graham Bell in Brantford and Baddeck NS built on that principle. How do you create power? Edison's power was DC, not AC.

An early power generating station developed in Niagara Falls, Canada and was owned by US Niagara Mohawk power system. It sold power to the US. Buffalo NY was illuminated by Canadian power generation! An Ontario power station opened in 1904 It had eleven 10,000 horsepower generating units, the largest at the time. It was decommissioned when the Beck Queenston generating station opened in 1917.

Fortunately, Canada was well-poised to develop power through its waterfalls. Enter Adam Beck of Baden, Ontario. He was a manufacturer who was elected mayor of

Beck 2 Generating Station

London ON, later an elected Conservative member of the Ontario Legislature and then named to Cabinet. James Whitney, the premier of Ontario, appointed him "Power Minister" in his Cabinet.

Beck set about to create a 110,000 volt transmission line from Niagara Falls to several municipalities in southern Ontario, including Toronto. On 11 October 1910 Adam Beck pulled the switch to inaugurate illumination in the region where he was born, at Berlin, now named Kitchener. For that accomplishment, King George V knighted him.

Beck's first hyper-hydroelectric power station of 1917 was the largest construction project ever undertaken in the region. It became a 450-megawatt power station at Queenston ON. Twenty-five years after his death, the government honoured Beck by naming the power station after him – "Beck 1." At that time, it was the world's largest power station. In 1950, another hydroelectric generating station was built along side it, employing 7,000 construction workers. It is called "Beck 2."

Americans followed suit in 1963, opening the Robert Moses Generating Station to supply energy to New York State.

The Genesis of GM
Enniskillen is a wine-producing and sheep-raising hamlet an hour-plus drive east of Toronto. Robert McLaughlin and his sons George and Robert Samuel (b. 08 Sept. 1871) lived here. Sam was more in tune with modern times than his father, and saw that the carriage industry his father built would soon give way to the motor car.

The McLaughlin Carriage Works factory burned down in 1899, giving Sam the opportunity to persuade his father and brother to manufacture automobiles. They began in 1908 by making bodies for William Durant, and when Durant added a Chevrolet line in 1918, the McLaughlins made bodies for them too in Oshawa, Ontario, south and east of their Enniskillen homes.

General Motors bought the McLaughlin company and formed General Motors Canada. Sam became president. He became vice president of the parent company. By 1926, the Oshawa ON-centred company employed 3,000 workers, producing the McLaughlin Buick and the Chevrolet for Canadians and the British Commonwealth market. Other lines were added gradually.

The McLaughlin Buick had a quality reputation, so when King George VI visited Canada in June 1939, a McLaughlin Buick squired the King and his Queen Elizabeth around Southern Ontario. The centenarian "Sam Mac," as he was sometimes called informally (but not to his face), became a great Canadian philanthropist.

Other companies saw the value of automobile manufacturing in Canada goading Ford to develop a major factory in Oakville ON and Fiat-Chrysler Corporation in Brampton ON.

Soldiering

Winston Churchill was likely the most noted participant in the Boer War (1898–1902) but Canadians also participated on the British side. French Canadians, in particular, objected to Canada's providing their youth to fight "for Britain." Some anglos in Canada also objected.

Great Britain asked Prime Minister Wilfrid Laurier's government to come alongside. He reluctantly agreed to authorize recruiting up to 1,000 soldiers for the cause. They were designated as the Second Special Service Battalion, the Royal Canadian Regiment.

Another 6,000 volunteers joined them, sailing for South Africa at the end of October 1899. Yet another 1,000 Canadian troops relieved 1,000 British troops stationed in Halifax, so they could be discharged and travel to the war zone.

Despite some citizens' initial misgivings about Canada's entry into that war, the final result engendered pride in many Canadians. Casualties were 224 Canadian dead, but half of these were felled by enteric fever disease. A monument to the veterans is erected on University Avenue in Toronto. Four Canadians received the Victoria Cross. The Peace of Vereeniging was signed 31 May 1902.

In June 1914, in Sarajevo, a young Gavrilo Princip Slavic nationalist, assassinated the Archduke Franz Ferdinand. He was heir to the throne of the Austrian-

Hungary Empire. This lit the fire, already smoking in the Balkans, where political intrigue was seething.

Because of negotiated, signed pacts, that murder brought Britain and France into a conflict, opposite Germany in the autumn of 1914. Canadians, still considered loyal and colonial by Britain, supported the British and quickly sent an Expeditionary Force.

By the end of 1914, 50,000 Canadians were enrolled, and by mid-1915, the number jumped to 150,000. The number gradually rose past 330,000. At first, the Canadian soldiers served under the command of the British army, often armed with defective Canadian-made Ross rifles. By mid-1915, the defective rifles were trashed.

Canadians soon demanded having control of their own army. That proved vital and resulted in a costly victory for Canadians at Vimy Ridge in 1917, something of a turning point in the war. At Vimy Ridge alone, Canada suffered 10,602 casualties with 3,598 dead among them. The entry of American soldiers in 1917 encouraged the allies and the US troops helped to end the war on 11 November 1918.

Canada lost 60,661 soldiers, airmen and sailors during the war. The Treaty of Versailles was signed by all parties on 28 June 1918. For a great read on the end of the war, get Gene Smith's, *When the Cheering Stopped*.

By 1939 Canada needed no invitation to fight Nazis in the Second World War. This time Canada sided with Great Britain not as a colony but as a fully independent nation. But Canada was poorly resourced pre-war – only 10 Bren guns! By the end of the war Canada had the third largest navy in the world, a huge merchant marine, a viable air force and a well-trained army. Over 40% of Canadian males ages 18–45 served in the Canadian armed forces, nearly all volunteers. 10% of all Canadians were in the armed services.

Canada served as a training facility of pilots for all Commonwealth nations entered in the war, and as an organizer of dangerous convoys ferrying materiel and food to the British Isles.

Some Canadian soldiers were trapped in Hong Kong when the Japanese forces captured it on Christmas Day, 1941. Some barely survived their imprisonment.

During the WWII, Canadian forces fought in the Battle of Britain, Raid on Dieppe, the D-Day Juno Beach invasion of Normandy, North African battles against the German General Erwin Rommel, the invasion of Sicily and Italy, the invasion of Germany, Belgium and Holland. Canadians were mostly responsible for liberating Holland.

WWII Casualties: Army–24,870 dead (505 died while POW), 58,094 wounded; Air Force–17,974 dead (49 died while POW); Navy–4,154 dead.

Canadian factories made bullets and bombs, rifles, canons and machine guns, built tanks, Liberator bombers, Spitfire fighters and Mosquito fighter-bombers.

Canadians fought in Korea, the Balkans (Bosnia) and the NATO-led invasion of Iraq (not the later US/UK invasion) and Afghanistan. Each war had casualties.

The Arrow

Canadians dared to plan a supersonic fighter plane which would be superior to any other in the world. Avro Canada began the design of the CF–105 Arrow in 1953. It would be a delta wing interceptor capable of near Mach 2 speed at altitudes of 50,000 feet (15,000 m). It would use

Orenda Iroquois engines and would serve The Royal Canadian Air Force (replica shown).

The Arrow's first flight was on 25 March 1958. Five Arrows were completed. Canada's problem was that it had a fighter plane far superior to any other in NATO, probably even better, some argue, than the renowned McDonnell Douglas F18 Hornet, but no one would buy it.

The issue came at a time of serious recession in Canada's economy. Prime Minister The Rt. Hon. John

Arrow Replica

George Diefenbaker's Cabinet determined that the debt involved in financing this remarkable jet would seriously affect Canada's economic position. On 20 February 1958, with many heavy hearts, angst and deep regret, the government cancelled the project with five planes built, tested and tried with a sixth 97% complete.

Canada's Cabinet ordered that existing planes be destroyed and all the blueprints scrapped. In the early-2010s, some volunteers rebuilt a model from preserved photos and placed the model in a museum.

That cancellation put many highly-trained, expert aeronautical engineers out of work. Many of them resurfaced with NASA in the USA and contributed greatly to space exploration. But it devastated the Canadian aeronautic industry. Gradually, the Canadian engineers found hope in Canada, especially with the rise of the Bombardier company.

Extending the Atlantic into the Midwest

The opening of the Welland Canal was a first step in future transportation of goods along Canada's waterways. The St. Mary's River near Sault Ste. Marie (Michigan and Ontario) had too many rapids for ships to deal with. (Sault is a French word for rapids).

The USA and Canada had warmer relations by the time the US Sault Ste. Marie (Soo) locks were opened in 1855. With larger ships and mechanical improvements, several US locks followed. International ships use it. Canada also built a smaller lock for recreational and tour ship use, opening in 1998.

The large lakers and "salties" had infrequently been using the Davis Lock, 411 m long (1,350 ft) since 1919. The mainly used MacArthur Lock was built in 1943 and is 800 ft (244 m long, 80 ft / 24 m wide and 29.5 ft /9 m deep).

A new "superlock" groundbreaking ceremony was held on 30 June 2009. The Soo Locks are a vital link in the development of the St. Lawrence Seaway.

Canada and USA launch St. Lawrence Seaway

With international trade exploding, Canadian and American governments realized the need for both lakers and ocean ships ("salties") to reach the Atlantic Ocean and vice versa. Negotiations, then plans developed to build channels where previously rapids hindered navigation along the St. Lawrence River.

A Canadian-US Deep Waterways Commission started the process but not without interference from

74

railways who had their own vested interests. Much of the proposed passageway was in Canada, some was within joint jurisdiction. The cost of the project was $470.3 million, of which Canada anted $336.5 million and the US, $133.8 million (*Seaway logo above*).

New channels were dug, four Montreal bridges were altered, existing channels were dredged, rapids were bypassed and much Canadian land expropriated (100 square miles; 259 sq. kms) and flooded. Some 6,500 people were displaced to form new communities of Long Sault, Ingleside and Iroquois in Ontario. Along with the Seaway, multiple installations became sources of hydroelectric power.

The first ship to use the Seaway was the icebreaker *D'Iberville* on 25 April 1959. On 26 June 1959, Queen Elizabeth II, Canadian Prime Minister John Diefenbaker, and US President Dwight D. Eisenhower officially dedicated the Seaway.

The next day, a ceremony was duplicated at Messina NY with the Queen and vice-president Richard Nixon taking part. Today, all traffic on the Seaway is computer controlled and the St. Lawrence Seaway is showing its considerable investment value.

Chapter Nine

The Welland Canal

The War of 1812 was a strong factor in protecting and enlarging Canada's trading routes. The day of portaging freight on great canoes was long past. Canadian visionaries set themselves to imagining what could be done to securely transfer freight from Lake Erie to Lake Ontario and vice versa.

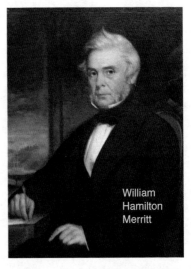

William Hamilton Merritt

William Hamilton Merritt, an entrepreneur operating a mill on Twelve Mile Creek near St. Catharine's, sought a channel to provide a reliable water supply for his mill. He proposed diverting water from the Welland River to his mill. An 1818 survey ensued, funded by Upper Canada at a cost of £2,000. The survey didn't satisfy Merritt's needs because it proposed a route bringing water from the Grand River to the municipality of Hamilton.

That was not good enough for Merritt. He mused about a water source to do double duty, provide for his own mill but also for securely transporting ships between Lake Erie and Lake Ontario. He launched his own survey in 1823, and in 1824, with associates, formed and incorporated the

Welland Canal Company. They raised £40,000 to begin the project.

By 1825, the 40-lock first canal was under construction at Allanburg. Underfunded and short of necessary water, the engineers had to funnel additional water from the Grand River after all. Despite these setbacks, on 30 November 1829, the first Welland Canal opened with the schooner *Anne and Jane* moving from Port Dalhousie on Lake Ontario to Buffalo on Lake Erie.

Evidence of the first canal is still visible near Allanburg. The canal was sabotaged at one point, dynamited by a shady felon, suspected as being the infamous Irish-American anarchist Mr. Benjamin Lett who destroyed the first monument to Isaac Brock. The lock was repaired.

Upper Canada's government noted the impecunity of the Welland Canal Company Inc. and in the general malaise of Upper Canada's post-war economy, bought shares in the company in 1839 and completed the transaction in 1841.

Remnants of the Third Welland Canal

It was now a public enterprise. A new canal was also necessary. Ships grew larger. The 40 locks were too many and required dredging. The second canal had 27 locks and opened in 1848. The new Erie and Ontario Railway gave the canal competition but only with small freight.

A third Welland Canal opened in 1887 with fewer locks capable of lifting larger ships. The ships were becoming still bigger and wider. A threat to the canal came by a trio of saboteurs – again with gaelic connections. A charge was set off east of the present Lock 7. The abandoned locks of this third Welland canal are still visible near and southeast of Lock 3 (see photo).

The felons were seen by a 16-year old girl. And caught! Ringleader "Dynamite" Luke Dillon, John Walsh (eventually released) and John Nolan were tried and sentenced in the Welland Court House. They were found guilty and received "life" sentences. The damaged parts were quickly repaired.

The fourth and present Welland Ship Canal is planned for replacement by 2030 but it has served shipping well since 1932. It has eight locks, each large enough to handle lakers and ocean ships. The depth is 26.5 ft (8.1 m), locks 766 ft (233.5 m) long. Each lock is 80 ft (24.4 m) wide. The largest ships that can use the canal are 740 feet (225.6 m) long. They carry a multitude of cargoes from oil to iron ore to stone and wheat. The ships serve several ports on Lakes Erie, St. Clair, Michigan, Huron and Superior. Thus they reach Cleveland, Toledo, Detroit, Chicago, Duluth, Sault Ste. Marie and Thunder Bay and several other ports.

Locks 4, 5 and 6 are double height locks and do the heaviest lifting. Two ships at a time can use these three locks. The other locks are single. A ship repair dry dock

Lock Seven, Welland Canal

facility is near Lock 1 and refurbishes the ships during the winter layover. Each ship is assigned a pilot to guide the ship through the entire canal. Private boating is allowed on the Welland Ship Canal but smaller craft must line up so that more than one occupies a lock at any one time.

Each lock takes 11–15 minutes to fill or empty. An arrester drops behind or before the ship to prevent it from crashing into the lock's gates. Tourist observation points are available at Lock 3 (best) with an observation platform, and Lock 7, the last lift over the Niagara Escarpment.

The Canal is 27 miles (43 km) long and takes about 11 hours to pass through. The height differential between the lakes Erie (at Port Colbourne) and (at Port Weller) Ontario is 326.5 feet (99.5 m). Ships carry 40,000,000 tonnes each year through the canal in 3,000 vessels

The Welland Ship Canal is now operated by the St. Lawrence Seaway Management Corporation.

Delicious Niagara Cherries

Chapter Ten

Soils and Crops

The Niagara area is blessed with excellent soil and a moderate climate. Along the plain of older glacial Lake Iroquois and the present-day plain of Lake Ontario sit the fertile soils of sand and clay left by the retreating glaciers.

The good rich soil of the Niagara area allows farmers to produce several kinds of tender fruits. First among its products are grapes of many varieties. They end up as wine, grape juice, preserves, and table grapes – and there are copious amounts of all these. In the clay loam areas, apples and pears use the nutrients in the soil for bountiful, nourishing products. In the sandy loam soil, the fruit with pits find a home – peaches, nectarines, plums and sweet cherries. They too come in abundance.

Niagara Grapes

These soils developed over time as the climate changed and hardwood forests mixed with the glacial soils. They are known as grey-brown podzols – dark on top leading to light brown underneath. These top layers of soil are slightly acidic. The lowest layer below them are alkilinic because of the rock layer being limestone (calcium carbonate). Perhaps a gardener should go to a rock quarry to get a pail of crushed and powdered dolomite to neutralize the soil around a favourite home maple tree.

As noted, the sandy loam soils provide nourishment for tender fruits such as sweet cherries, peaches and apricots (the "stone pit" fruits). Clay loam soils are ideal for "seed fruit," such as apples and pears. Grapes grow in both kinds of soil. Grasses primarily grow in clay loams, and so cattle are raised where these grasses predominate, mainly above the Escarpment.

It seems that the grape varieties predominate the fruit areas, because the revenue created exceeds profits derived from tender fruits. Wineries are ubiquitous in this plain as is evidenced from Niagara-on-the-Lake's 125 wineries.

This is due to variations in

Gary Pilliteri of Pilliteri Winery

good soil, drafts from currents travelling down the Escarpment and the proximity to Lake Ontario. These factors help reduce frost, or alternatively, delay the blossoming until the frost period passes.

Niagara Peaches

Niagara leads the world in the production of ice wine. The wine is produced when some grapes remain on the vine until four frosty days in late December or early January. The grapes are then harvested, sometimes at night, after temperatures in the area drop below minus eight celsius (–8 C) for a few days. The cost increases directly as more pickers work overtime. Wineries process the frozen grapes which produce a very sweet wine.

Spring grape growth at Pilliteri Winery

Chapter Eleven

Bridges and Trade

Canada and the United States of America each trade more with each other than with any other nation. Much of that trade crosses the mutual boundaries in the Niagara Peninsula. Trade traverses the Niagara River by both train and truck.

Former Bridges

The history of bridges spanning the Niagara River goes back to the mid 1800s. Time and wear have made the earliest efforts obsolete.

The exceptions are a railway bridge connecting Fort Erie, Ontario with Buffalo, New York and the Niagara Gorge Railway bridge connecting Niagara Falls and its opposite city across the border. Both spans are still in use.

By 1845, officials realized the importance of constructing a bridge at Niagara Falls. Planners and engineers went to work, and when they finished, produced a suspension bridge. Charles Ellet offered a prize of $5.00 for any child who could fly a kite from the US to Canada.

One lad succeeded. The kite string towed a small steel wire, replaced by a thicker wire until a wire cable over a half inch thick connected the two countries. But it carried only a small load, a basket carrying two people across the river. Obviously, that was only a start and not a very satisfactory one at that.

There followed a suspension bridge built close to the Falls. It had two decks 28 feet (2.6 m) apart, one for train traffic and one for horse carriages, cattle, and people. The

83

bridge was the world's first railway bridge and was operational from 1855 for 42 more years. It was replaced in 1997. A new version is known as the Whirlpool Rapids Bridge. It remains in use.

Entrepreneurs erected a third bridge across the Niagara River at Queenston. It was opened in 1855 and lasted until 1864 when gale winds destroyed it.

This suspension Queenston–Lewiston Bridge was 845 feet (78.5 m) long. It hung from two stone towers imbedded and anchored into solid rock on each side of the river. Ten humungous cables suspended the roadway.

The "Honeymoon" Bridge opened near the Falls in 1898. The carriage and pedestrian span at Niagara Falls suffered a complete collapse on 23 January 1938 when massive ice slabs from Lake Erie piled up, destroying the supports.

It was replaced in two years' time by the present Rainbow Bridge, slightly downstream, further north.

Rainbow Bridge: Canada to USA

Niagara Gorge Railway and Automobile Nexus Bridge

As noted previously, the two level railway Bridge remains useful. Passenger trains connecting Toronto Union Station and New York pass each way about once a day.

Freight traffic is much more frequent. Passenger cars, but not buses are permitted on the lower road deck roadway only for those bearing Nexus IDs.

Nexus is a security-clearance program that permits those possessing the ID to cross the international border with less red tape or immigration examination. Nexus works well on this crossing but not quite as well on the busier bridges at the Peace Bridge or especially Queenston–Lewiston.

The Peace Bridge, Fort Erie

Before the Peace Bridge was opened, a railway bridge a short distance to the north, was opened and remains

Railway / Lower Arch Bridge and White Water Walk

operational. The Grand Trunk Railway supported the construction. It opened in 1873. It spanned 1,113 m or 3,651 feet and had only one rail line.

The Peace Bridge was so named to celebrate peace between the two countries for 100 years since the War of 1812–1814. It connects the City of Buffalo and the Town of Fort Erie. It is located 20 kilometres (12.4 miles) south of Niagara Falls. The bridge span is 1,768 m (5,800 ft).

When the Peace Bridge was officially opened on 01 June 1927, several dignitaries honoured the dedication with their presence. Included in the guest list were the Prince of Wales (later to become King Edward VIII); Canadian Prime Minister William Lyon Mackenzie King; US Vice President Charles Dawes; New York Governor Al Smith; Ontario Premier Howard Ferguson; and the UK's Prime Minister Stanley Baldwin.

This is a key bridge for truck traffic. Over 4,000 trucks cross here every day. Passenger traffic is also busy. Electronic signs placed a few miles or kilometres before the bridge announce if there are delays, and if so, an estimate for line-up times.

Tolls for the Peace Bridge are collected on the Canadian side. Plans for a new twin bridge are under consideration.

Rainbow Bridge

The collapse of the Honeymoon Bridge in 1938 left no option but to replace it. Fortunately, planners had previously decided that it was outmoded, so specs were already underway. The span is 286 m (940 ft)

The plans were speeded up, so that by the time King George VI and Queen Elizabeth arrived for their June, 1939

Royal Tour, the completed span was ready for them to dedicate it. Americans also had dignitaries present. Since Canada was only three months away from being at war with Germany, the vital link to the USA was essential. It officially opened for traffic on 01 November 1941.

Today, no trucks are allowed on this bridge. It is strictly for autos, motorcycles and pedestrians. It is busy, but wait times are usually less than at the Peace Bridge.

Engineers have developed ways to prevent further ice jams on the Niagara River, so that challenge is unlikely to occur again as it did with the Honeymoon Bridge.

Queenston–Lewiston Bridge

The same bridge architect, Richard Su Min Lee, who designed the Rainbow Bridge, also designed the newer Queenston–Lewiston Bridge, 10 kilometres (six miles) downstream. Its location is very near the starting point of the Niagara Escarpment, where once the Falls began as the ice retreated about 12,000 years ago.

It replaced the previous bridge which, in 1864, "blew down" near this place. The new bridge is a short distance upstream and better located.

No pedestrians may cross here but taxis and trucks make much use of it. It opened 01 November 1969 and much relieved the serious truck traffic issues on these four busy international crossings.

The bridge is next to two of Niagara's power stations, the Robert Moses Power Generating Station in New York and the Beck I and II Power Generating Stations in Ontario. This bridge effectively serves traffic heading east and south to the New York toll highway to New York City – or in reverse if entering Canada.

Visiting Mighty Niagara

This five-lane bridge spans 488 m, or 1,600 ft. The bridge clears the river by 113 m or 370 ft It is maintained by both countries through the joint Niagara Falls Bridge Commission.

International Control Structure above the Falls

Chapter Twelve

Maintaining a Beautiful Environment

Niagara Parkway Mandate

Visitors to Niagara Falls are astonished at its pristine ambience. God allowed natural forces to form the fantastic Falls but humans are the responsible stewards of the Niagara environment.

You won't find litter strewn around the Niagara Parkway. What you do see is a prudently planned parkland for visitors to celebrate completely. Niagara attractions do not just happen; they all come under the design and guidance of the Niagara Parkway Commission (NPC).

The NPC operates with a dozen commissioners, eight of whom are appointed and four elected from its neighbouring communities. It regulates its jurisdiction very carefully.

The Commission began in 1885 and is completely self-funding. It is responsible to the Ontario Government through the Ministry of Tourism, Culture and Sport. It operates at no cost to taxpayers.

Its revenues derive from restaurants, gift shops, parking, golf courses, and the Parkway's many attractions. From this budget it provides its own police force, garbage collection, fire department, bus transit, engineering, and horticultural displays.

How Can You Enjoy What the NPC Offers?

Visitors may maximize their visit by purchasing a Multi-Attraction Event Adventure Pass; These come in three forms: (1) a classic pass offering six themes; and (2) a nature pass of six themes; (3) a Niagara Heritage Trail Pass (Old Fort Erie, Mackenzie Printery, Laura Secord Homestead, McFarland House).

First, park your car in the safe NPC designated parking lot. It costs a small amount but a bus will save you parking elsewhere. Parkway parking is scarce until you reach Brock's monument where parking is free.

Next, take the WEGO bus. Its circuit includes the main southern parking lot and extends north to Brock's Monument National Park. A ticket allows you to visit several important stops along the way. With the pass, you can get off and on the bus at each important attraction. You may buy a one day or two day pass. The following suggestions are important items to enhance your Niagara visit.

From Brock's Monument, driving north to Niagara-on-the-Lake is relatively easy. Parking is no problem at the various stops, except for meters in NOTL on the streets and a flat rate meter at Fort George.

- **Hornblower Cruise.** Take the one-of-a-kind boat on a one-of-a-kind dazzling journey right up to the base of the Falls. The 700-passenger, state-of-the-art catamaran replaces the dated *Maid of the Mist* which now operates only on the American side. Reservations are timed. The season ends about 24 October.

- **School of Horticulture.** The school operates on a three-year program, two years in residence. It prepares plants, shrubs and trees to maintain the entire Parkway. Its Botanical Gardens are located on a 100 acre (40 hectare) park, offering visitors a leisurely stroll through its unique arboretum and manicured gardens of shrubs and roses. A new Legacy Garden opened in 2014, paying tribute to graduates of the School. The theme of the Park is "Biodiversity and Sustainability." It is free to visitors each day from dawn to dusk. Nearby parking is not free but the cost is nominal.

Newly Emerged Butterfly

- **Butterfly Conservatory.** The building for the beautiful butterflies is adjacent to the School of Horticulture. Parking is $5.00 for visitors, unless you are on a coach tour and have designated and paid for this stop before you arrived in Niagara Falls. Each morning, the keepers introduce 2,000 newly emerged butterflies into the tropical atmosphere of the Conservatory. The parking lot is shared with visitors to the School of Horticulture.

- **Parks: Queen Victoria Park** parallels the Niagara River along the parkway from the Horseshoe Falls to the American Falls. The park honours Queen Victoria, who was the monarch of the British Empire when the NPC initiated the park. It is a walking and "sitting" park, replete with wonderful seasonal flower displays and shade trees. Its ambience provides a suitable setting for picnics.

- **Oakes Garden Theatre** and **Japanese Garden** is across the road, north from Queen Victoria Park and also overlooks the American Falls. The Oakes Garden Theatre is amphitheatre-shaped, flowing down from decorative columns in a curved arch in well-trimmed lawn to its base. The Japanese Garden at the northern upper level of the Garden Theatre has a distinct Japanese flavour to it, replete with shade trees, delicate flowers, a little bridge over a brook and a fish pond.

- **Queenston Heights.** This park has a beautiful walking area, a large spread of manicured lawn, flowerbeds, picnic tables, a restaurant and washrooms. It provides a great view of the place where the Escarpment began 12,000 years ago, and its plaques tell of the battle layout of 13 October 1812. A plaque also honours the "Coloured Corps," a group of "black" soldiers who took part in the Battle of Queenston Heights. The main focus, of course, is the monument which stands over the grave of Sir Isaac. You may climb to the top if you wish (a small fee). NPC maintains the park; Parks Canada maintains the monument.

- Stroll in the NOTL **Queen's Royal Park** at Ricardo Street at the southern shore of Lake Ontario. The attractive gazebo in the park is a "donation" leftover from the 1983 movie, *The Dead Zone*, from Stephen King's novel. To the east, the Niagara River flows north into Lake Ontario.

Across the river is Fort Niagara in New York. It was built originally by the French, then captured by the British after 1759 and eventually ceded to the USA. You will find benches and picnic tables. You may spot a wedding here.

• **Falls Incline Railway.** In 1966 the NPC introduced the Incline Railway to transport visitors between the Fallsview tourist area and Table Rock. In 2014, it was revamped and enlarged. It carries up to 1,000 passengers in an hour. The plexiglass-topped cars take one minute to cover the 50 meter (165 ft) drop.

• **Parkway Walks and Trails.** The Niagara River Recreation Trail is a paved pathway next to, and overlooking the Niagara River. It covers 33 miles (53 kms) from Fort Erie to Niagara-on the-Lake at Fort George. It is suitable for walking, biking, jogging and even wheelchairs. The trail links Niagara-on-the-Lake with Niagara Falls and Fort Erie.

• Half-way between the ends of the trail it links with the southern terminus of the Bruce Trail. This walking and hiking (also camping) trail follows the Escarpment west and north past Hamilton right to its northern terminus at Tobermory on Lake Huron and Georgian Bay. The Bruce Trail is part of a Canada-wide hiking trail of 10,000 miles (15,000 kms.) touching on the Atlantic, Pacific and Arctic Oceans. Quite a walk!

• An easier walk is within the Dufferin Islands just south of the Falls nearby the upper rapids. This nature area honours Lord Dufferin, once the Governor General of Canada. Eleven foot bridges mark the islands and allow walkers opportunity to examine the flora and fauna of the nature preserve.

- **Golf.** If golf is your "thing," Niagara Parks scratches your itch. The attractive Whirlpool Golf Course (with a delightful public restaurant attached to it) opened in 1950 and offers an 18-hole challenge. It is 10 minutes north of the Falls.
- South, in Chippawa, near where the historic 1814 battle was fought, designers have turned swords into ploughshares, well, golf courses. The Legends of Niagara complex has 45 holes in all, two 18-holers (Usher's Creek) (Battlefield), and one nine-holer. These courses were created by golf architects Doug Carrick and Thomas McBroom. Here is also a driving range. The courses boast an excellent restaurant and a banquet hall.
- Near the Park headquarters at Oak Hall, golfers will find a par three, nine-hole course.

- **Niagara Helicopters.** Catch a fantastic view of the Falls and Niagara Gorge by taking a helicopter ride. It considerably changes your perspective of the Falls, the Whirlpool Aero Car, and White Water rapids. Free parking. Family and group rates. Visit the heliport on 3731 Victoria Avenue at the Niagara River Parkway [905-357-5672].

- **Enjoyment.** You can spend a lot of time just plain enjoying yourself in Niagara Falls. You have spaces to stroll, picnic and cycle. Just sit and watch the scenery. If you gamble, you may visit the casinos at the Falls. If you win, you will enjoy the chancy experience; if you lose,

Niagara Helicopters

your anticipated enjoyment will quickly dissipate. Or, you can just watch others win or lose.

- Each Friday, sometimes Wednesdays and on national holidays, weather permitting, Queen Victoria Park offers free fireworks (10:00 pm). Go to the Illumination Tower at 8:00 pm for free concert Sunday evenings and on holidays mid-May through Labour Day. See the Falls lit up in colour by the 21 Xenon lights. They are 30 inches (76 centimetres) in diameter. Look for 18 of them at the Illumination Tower beside Queen Victoria Park. The other three lights are near the base of the Falls close to the gorge at the American Falls. They produce 250 million candlepower and use different colour combinations.

- **Clifton Hill Amusements.** Some visitors to Niagara Falls like what we call kitschy entertainment, a upside-down house and the like. Not all of Clifton Hill is kitschy. It has mini-golf, bowling, good eateries, a midway, Wax Museum, Guinness World Records, Haunted House, Lego

Brick City, a Mystery Maze, House of Frankenstein, Crystal Caves, Indoor Skydiving, Arcade with 300 games, Go-Karts, and the Niagara SkyWheel. Is that enough choice?

• **Skylon Tower.** The tower is located at 5200 Robinson Street [905-356-2651]. It offers the best observation lookout in the area. On a clear day you easily can see the Toronto skyline to the north. Except for a helicopter ride, it also gives the prime view of the Falls, the upper Niagara River rapids, various locations in the city of Niagara Falls ON and NY. It has two great restaurants, one a revolving dining room, the other a summit suite buffet menu. Dinner includes free elevation to the Observation deck. Tourist items are available at each of the restaurants, one on the main floor, another on the lowest floor. An amusement arcade is in the lower section.

• **Imax.** School chums from Galt Collegiate Institute in Galt, Ontario dreamed up a new way to film and show movies. They were Robert Kerr, Graeme Ferguson and Bill Shaw. They envisioned and created Imax in Canada. They offered their invention to Expo '67 in Montreal and then in 1970 to Japan's Expo. The rest is history. There is no place with a better location to show off the Imax one-hour performance than in Niagara Falls. It is a dynamic way of viewing all that Niagara area offers. Imax uses a 60-foot screen with dynamic digital sound and offers its presentation in eight languages. It is located close to the Skylon Tower. Combined with Imax is a Daredevil Museum at the Fallsview Casino.

Whirlpool Aerocar

- **Whirlpool Aerocar.** Sometimes it's called the Spanish Aero Car. That's because a Spanish engineer designed this exciting attraction, first opening in 1916. For a century the Aero Car has transported passengers over the unique whirlpool. The cable car transports people from Colts Point to Thomson Point, both points in Canada. The car rides on six cables (yes, it's safe) for 1,770 ft (539 m) and 250 ft (76.2 m) suspended above the seething water of the whirlpool. The whirlpool dissipates at night when some water flowing over the Falls is diverted to created power generation at the Beck 1 and 2 Power plants down river.

- **Table Rock.** Table Rock, at the brink of the Horseshoe Falls offers a fantastic view of the Falls, but also some great attractions, tourist mementoes, good dining at Elements, and reasonably priced fast food – a burger stop and Tim Horton's (coffee, soup, sandwich etc.). This is

Journey Behind The Falls

where Nik Wallenda arrived on his 2013 tightrope walk across the Falls.

- **Journey Behind the Falls.** Within the Table Rock you will find the entrance to The Journey Behind the Falls. For a modest fee you can elevate to a passage way behind the Falls and watch the water from behind the Falls. Or you can walk outside very close to the Falls and watch the water come close by you. A necessary raincape is provided (free).

- **Niagara's Fury.** Have you wondered how the Falls was formed? Niagara's Fury will help to provide an answer. Enter the program at Table Rock. When you first enter, you will see a showing of animated woodland creatures explaining the ice age and how it impacted Niagara Falls. Following the eight-minute introduction, you are transported into a 360-degree theatre. Temperatures drop. Water bubbles spray and snow falls around you. You stand in a mist and suddenly feel the huge platform shake and tilt as you experience the evolution of the Falls.

- **Floral Showhouse.** Slightly south of the Falls, and near the upper rapids, is the Floral Showhouse, open year-round. It is an explosion of colour, and the flowers are changed eight times a year. To add to the visual impact, some 70 tropical songbirds fly freely and live in the building's tropical displays. NPC provides signs in Braille for the visually impaired. A rose garden lies outside the Showhouse. It blooms at the appropriate times of the summer and fall.

- **White Water Walk.** Just north of the Whirlpool Bridge is the entry to the Niagara Gorge. NPC calls it the White Water Walk, and for good reason. All the water going over the Falls is channeled through this gorge and it takes your breath away to see it. The walk features a "class six" rapids, the highest level recorded. The gorge is less than 310 ft (95 m) wide, so the Niagara River runs about 25–30 mph as it rushes north toward the whirlpool and Lake Ontario. You reach the rapids by elevator, and then hike along the boardwalk for 300 m (1,000 ft) to view the sight. Along the boarded path are many items of information about the geology and historic facts involving the gorge.

- **Laura Secord Homestead.** Laura Ingersoll Secord was one of Canada's true heroes, recognized by a statue at Canada's cenotaph in Ottawa. She was born in Great Barrington, Massachusetts and emigrated to Canada with

Queenston: Laura Secord Homestead

many others who preferred British governance. With her husband, they became established merchants in Queenston. Her husband James, a sergeant in the British army, and a United Empire Loyalist, was severely wounded at the Queenston Heights combat. Laura Secord nursed him back to health in their home. A half-year later , 12 June 1813, she overheard the American soldiers who had commandeered their home, discussing the next day's battle plans. Immediately, she hiked 17 miles (27 kms) over various paths until she reached the British contingent stationed at Beaver Dams near Thorold. When the US forces arrived, the British and Natives were ready for them and easily won the day. Laura Secord also lived for a while in Chippawa. A church building on the Queenston premises is used for weddings and similar purposes.

- **Mackenzie Printery.** William Lyon Mackenzie set up a printing press here to promote his "democratic" ideas in

The Mackenzie Printery

his *Colonial Advocate*. McMaster U. and York U. history professor William Kilbourn labelled him, "*The Firebrand*" in a book of that name. After a self-enforced exile in the US because of a rebellion he led, Mackenzie eventually returned to Toronto and was elected as its first mayor. A descendant, William Lyon Mackenzie King became Prime Minister of Canada. The printery shows a 500-year variety of printing presses used when lead type was in vogue. The Printery is located at the foot of Queenston Heights within a couple of blocks of the Laura Secord Homestead.

- **McFarland House.** Along the River Road and just southeast of the Old Town (Niagara-on-the-Lake) is McFarland House. British troops used the residence as a hospital for a while. American invaders also used the facility as a hospital for a spell and partially destroyed it before retreating from Canada. However, the Georgian style brick dwelling has been resurrected as an example of a prosperous house in and about the year 1800. In the summer months, interpreters wearing period costumes guide and welcome visitors to hear about the residence and its place in Niagara's history. It provides a large pavilion suitable for picnics. Alternatively, a visitor may want to buy its offering of baked goods and enjoy a "spot" of tea on its Tea Garden patio.

- **Shaw Theatre.** This Niagara-on-the-Lake modern theatre offers world class presentations of dramas and musicals. The menu changes each year but musicals include (as an example) *Cabaret*, the 2014 musical offering. Dramas include plays in its Festival Theatre such as *Arms and the Man*, *The Cherry Orchard*, *Major Barbara*, The *Philadelphia Story*, and often some lesser known dramas performed on one of its smaller and more intimate stages at the Royal George, Court House and Studio theatres.

- **125 wineries.** Niagara-on-the-Lake has 125 wineries in its compact region below the Niagara Escarpment. Some wineries offer wine-tasting and some may allow you into their temperature-controlled cellars to see how the vintners make and keep the wine. The area is so blessed with good weather and excellent soil that wineries thrive. Most of the wineries compete well internationally. Pilliteri Winery, for example, produces 20% of the world's ice wine.

- **Whirlpool Jet Boat Tours.** If you want a thrilling ride on the Niagara River, try the jet boat ride from Niagara-on-the-Lake to the Whirlpool. The tour offers two types of

Whirlpool Jet Boat

boats, one with a dome to keep you dry and another open boat to let you feel the wind and perhaps the spray. For the "wet" tour bring a towel. Canada offers two locations, at 61 Melville Street in Niagara-on-the-Lake, and at 3850 Niagara Parkway at the Whirlpool.

- **NOTL Golf Course.** Golf enthusiasts may hone their game at the Niagara-on-the-Lake course near the former Fort Mississauga along the south shore of Lake Ontario. The course claims to be the oldest in North America, dating to 1875. It has nine holes.

- **Negro Burial Ground NOTL.**  Some former slaves found refuge and work in Niagara-on-the-Lake. They built a Baptist Church on a small lot at 494 Mississauga Street. The church building is long gone but a "Negro Burial Ground" has two headstones of former members of the church. You pass by it quickly if you are in too much of a hurry, so slow down. Canadian flags sometimes decorate the grave stones.

- **Chocolate FX Factory.** Many groups stop at the Chocolate FX Factory on 335 Four Mile Creek, close to St. David's and near to Regional Road 81. Group Tours are available if reservations are made. Most of the Factory's wholesale products are shipped out-of-country, usually bearing the name of the company buying the product. You will not see FX products under that name in retail shops but visitors may buy the products at the FX Factory.

- **Rossi Glass.** Glass-blowing and its beautiful creations may be seen and purchased at Rossi Glass in the Souvenir City Building at 4199 River Road (north from the Rainbow Bridge). It specializes in Cranberry Glass which requires some gold inserted in the glass blowing. You are invited to watch an artisan at work. Rossi Glass ships its products around the globe.

- **Secret Garden.** The Secret Garden is a combined lunch and coffee stop and an excellent souvenir shop with quality goods. It is located where the old bus station existed, north and next to the Japanese Garden and Oakes Theatre Garden. You can eat inside or alfresco. The view is outstanding, looking directly at the American Falls. It is next to the carillon, making it a great spot to relax during a recital, or to view the Falls at night when illuminated.

- **Carillon.** At the western side of the Rainbow bridge, above the custom and immigration booths for entrants to Canada, the Falls offers carillon recitals from time to time. The carillonneur plays on Sundays and holidays and on special occasions. The sound is wonderful. Maybe he'd play for your 50th Anniversary? Ask.

- **Marineland.** Marineland is a veteran amusement park in the Niagara area. Located at 7657 Portage Road, the park features rides and fun from mid-May to Canadian Thanksgiving (second Monday in October). The park offers bison, deer, elk, seals, dolphins, orcas, belugas. Buffet meal is available. Of course the park provides showtimes with sea animals doing their leaps and rolls. If you like rides, Marineland has more than a dozen of them from Ferris Wheel to Sky Screamer, varied from tame to adventurous. Camping is available. So is a season pass.

• **1812 War Battle sites.** Beaver Dams; Lundy's Lane; Queenston Heights; Chippawa Battle Ground; Old Fort Erie. (see Chapter seven)

• **Fort George, Old Fort Niagara.** In Niagara-on-the- Lake you can visit historic Fort George. This is a restoration, of course, since American troops razed it during the War of 1812–14. Canadian hero Major-General Sir Isaac Brock was buried here twice after being shot by an American sniper (later buried under Brock's Monument). The Fort is maintained by Parks Canada. The entrance fee is modest. The Fort offers a glimpse of officers' and regulars' quarters, the magazine, homestyle cooking of the day, and even a demonstration on firing an 1812 rifle. Children come here on day outings to learn about Canadian history. Its bookroom sells a variety of Canadian history books. You may be serenaded by a piper.

• **Floral Clock.** When you stop at the 40-foot foot (12-m) clock next to the Beck generating station, you will notice individuals and groups using the setting for a camera

background. What a backdrop! Over 15,000 flowers are used to enhance the clock. The floral themes change throughout the season.

- **Centennial Lilac Gardens.** In 1967, when Canada celebrated 100 years of confederation, the Rotary Clubs of New York State provided a lasting gift to Canada and the Niagara Parkway. You can see this gift in the form of a Lilac Garden, featuring 225 varieties of Lilac trees. It is nearby the Floral Clock. Lilacs flower any time from later April to early June. The display is awesome.

- **Museums.** The NOTL Historical Museum (43 Castlereigh St.) is a good way to learn about the town's rich and varied past. It offers good information on the arrival and presence of blacks who lived and worked in the village. In the city of Niagara Falls, the Niagara History Museum has records of many facets of the city's past. At 5810 Ferry St., the Lundy's Lane Historical Museum has a collection of Black History items. The Niagara area was a terminus on the Underground Railroad (at Buffalo, Queenston and NOTL) which helped escaping slaves to find freedom in Canada. A Lacrosse and Vintage Car Museum is located at Lock Three on the Welland Canal. Entrance is free but a donation gift is much appreciated.

- **Old Fort Erie.** The old Fort was reconstructed in 1937, revealing life at the time of the War of 1812–1814. Americans captured it twice and left it in ruins. It witnessed the heaviest casualties of the war. Now the Fort comes to life with guards and interpreters dressed in period costumes, and some "summer soldiers" showing how their weapons were fired. A small museum in the Old Fort show period items. A gift shop at the Fort is a good place to by a souvenir, or to enjoy a cup of coffee. The Fort opens in late May and closes mid-October.

A student summer guard meets visitors at Old Fort Erie, explaining the Fort's fascinating history

• **Tour of Beck 2 Generating Station.** The Beck Generating Station is available for short tours but they must be reserved. The tour fee is modest. You can see the penstocks and generators but for security reasons, the tour allows no entry to the main floor.

Visiting Mighty Niagara

notes:

Made in the USA
Charleston, SC
31 January 2016